ReviseandShine

KS2Maths

Simon Greaves, Helen Greaves and Anne Loadman

INTRODUCTION

In the weeks leading up to the National Tests, your child will be given practice tests and revision at school. However, many children benefit from doing extra revision at home. This book will help your child prepare for their National Test in Maths through a carefully planned eight-week revision period.

The book is divided into eight revision units. Each unit covers a whole week's work and for every day within that week there are two pages of content. The first page presents all the information your child needs to know in an interesting and friendly way, and the second page (the practice page), assesses their understanding of that information. The final part of the book contains a practice test (see page 81), following the format of the National Maths Test, as well as a comprehensive answer section (see page 92). Guidance is also given on how to award a level (see page 96).

Successful revision

The key to using this book successfully is to know the ability of your child. Although the book has been designed to fit an eight-week plan, it could just as successfully be spread over a longer time. However, covering the book in a shorter time is not advised, as each child needs time to develop the depth of knowledge required. You can use the checklist on page 4 to monitor progress and give your child a sense of achievement.

Be guided by the ability of your child and don't be tempted to rush. If you have covered a topic and they still seem unsure, move on but come back to the other topic later. Sometimes children need time to assimilate knowledge and understanding and what seemed impossible on one day, will seem easier on another. Always try to build on success.

Talk to your child about the content of the information pages, to make sure they are clear about all the terms before they attempt the practice pages. Clear up uncertainties as you go along.

Revision tips
- Regular and frequent revision is most effective.
- Don't try and cover too much at once.
- Focus on one topic at a time and go at your child's pace.
- Try not to feel frustrated if your child can't do or remember something.
- Reinforce correct answers by repeating the correct answer back to your child to show how they should be answering a particular question.
- Give hints and praise effort.

What are the National Tests?
The National Tests take place in May each year. The tests for KS2 are in English, Maths and Science and are administered over the course of a week. The National Test in Maths at KS2 is made up of three separate tests:

Test A – a written paper where calculators must not be used. This test lasts for 45 minutes and is worth 40 marks.

Test B – a written paper where calculators are allowed. This test lasts for 45 minutes and is worth 40 marks.

The **Mental test** contains 20 mental maths questions where calculators must not be used. The questions are read out on a tape and children have a few seconds to answer each question. This test lasts approximately 15 minutes and is worth 20 marks.

The questions in the tests cover Maths at Levels 3, 4 and 5. The tests may contain questions from any of the four main areas covered in maths lessons. These are number and algebra; shape, space and measures; working with data; problem solving.

The tests are marked by external examiners and the scripts are returned to the school at the beginning of July. The marks for each paper are totalled and a level is given, usually between 3 and 5. Level 4 is the average level to be achieved by an 11-year-old. It is important to note that the tests cannot be passed or failed. They measure the level at which your child is currently working.

CONTENTS

REVISION CHECKLIST

Numbers and the Number System	Page numbers	Revised
Place value	pages 5–6	
Ordering numbers	pages 7–8	
Rounding numbers	pages 9–10	
Properties of numbers	pages 27–28	
Number sequences	pages 29–30	
Equivalent fractions	pages 45–46	
Fractions of quantities	pages 47–48	
Percentages	pages 55–56	
Fractions, decimals and percentages	pages 57–58	
Ratio and proportion	pages 59–60	
Negative numbers	pages 65–66	
Calculations		
Addition calculations	pages 15–16	
Subtraction calculations	pages 17–18	
Using a calculator	pages 23–24	
Multiplication calculations	pages 25–26	
Division calculations	pages 35–36	
Multiplying and dividing (by 10, 100 and 1000)	pages 37–38	
Solving Problems		
Measures problems	pages 43–44	
Money problems	pages 63–64	
Time problems	pages 73–74	
Number and shape problems	page 75	
One-step problems	page 76	
Multi-step problems	page 77	
Reasoning about numbers	page 78	
Reasoning about shapes	page 79	
Investigating general statements	page 80	
Measures		
Units and their conversions	pages 39–40	
Using units	pages 41–42	
Perimeter and area	pages 61–62	
Time	pages 71–72	
Shape and Space		
Triangles and polygons	pages 11–12	
Quadrilaterals	pages 13–14	
Symmetry in 2-D shapes	pages 19–20	
3-D shapes	pages 21–22	
Angles	pages 31–32	
Position and direction	pages 67–68	
Reflection, rotation and translation	pages 69–70	
Handling Data		
Probability	pages 33–34	
Mode, median and mean	pages 49–50	
Diagrams, graphs and tables	pages 51–52	
Charts	pages 53–54	

PLACE VALUE

What you need to know

1 Understand the place value of whole numbers and decimals up to three decimal places.

2 Read and write numbers, including decimals, in words and figures.

3 Partition (split up) numbers into thousands, hundreds, tens, units, tenths, hundredths and thousandths.

PLACE VALUE OF WHOLE NUMBERS

- **Place value** means that each **digit** in a number has a value which depends on its position in the number.
- Each digit is worth 10 times **more** than the digit to its **right** and 10 times **less** than the digit to its **left**.
- A place value chart can be used to help work out the value of each digit in a number.

Notice that the 3 in 63 794 is 10 times bigger than the 3 in the number 387.

Example   Look at this number   63 794

millions	hundreds of thousands	tens of thousands	thousands	hundreds	tens	units
		6	3	7	9	4

6 **tens of thousands** + 3 **thousands** + 7 **hundreds** + 9 **tens** + 4 **units**

= 60 000   + 3000   + 700   + 90   + 4

= 63 794

or sixty three thousand, seven hundred and ninety-four

Notice that the 9 in 63 794 is 100 times smaller than the 9 in the number 9371.

DECIMAL NUMBERS

- The **decimal point** separates whole numbers from decimal fractions, e.g. **tenths**, **hundredths**, **thousandths**.
- For decimal numbers there are digits after the decimal point. These represent fractions of units.

Example   3·71

tens	units	tenths	hundredths	thousandths
	3	7	1	

3 units + 7 tenths + 1 hundredths

= 3   + 0·7   + 0·01

= 3·71

or three and seventy one hundredths

(say this number as three point seven one)

PLACE VALUE

1 Write these numbers in figures.

(a) Thirteen thousand, one hundred and fifty-seven [   ]

(b) Seven point five two [   ]

2 For each set of numbers, put a circle around the smallest number and underline the largest number.

(a) 3·12   2·123   3·123   3·012   3·001   2·312

(b) 12·95   11·06   12·45   11·98   12·02   11·13

3 Write the value of the number 3 in each of these numbers.

(a) 17 263   _____

(b) 1340   _____

(c) 59·3   _____

4 Here are four digit cards.   [0]   [9]   [5]   [1]

(a) What is the smallest number you can make using all four cards? [   ]

(b) What is the largest number you can make using all four cards? [   ]

5

Ian

Our school library has eight thousand and fifty-five books.

Jessica

Our school library has eight thousand, five hundred and five books.

Whose library has more books?

Circle either   **Jessica**   or   **Ian**

Write the largest number in figures.

[   ]   1 mark

TOTAL [   ]

ORDERING NUMBERS

What you need to know

1 Read and order whole and decimal numbers, including measures.

2 Compare numbers using words and symbols: <, >, ≤, ≥ and =.

3 Give a number which falls between any two numbers, including decimals.

ORDERING WHOLE NUMBERS

• Numbers may be ordered by comparing the place value of their digits.

Example: Which is the larger number: 12371 or 12731?
Compare these two numbers by studying the place value of each digit.

12371		**12731**
10000	← same number of tens of thousands →	10000
2000	← same number of thousands →	2000
300	greater number of hundreds →	700
70		30
1		1

so 12731 is larger than 12371
or 12731 is greater than 12371
or 12731 > 12371

ORDERING DECIMAL NUMBERS

• The same method can be used to arrange a list of decimal numbers or measures in either **ascending** order (from smallest to largest) or **descending** order (from largest to smallest).

Comparing numbers
These signs can be used to compare numbers:
< (**less than**)
> (**greater than**)
≤ (**less than or equal to**)
≥ (**greater than or equal to**)
= (**equal to**)

The widest part of the > sign always points towards the larger number.

ORDERING NUMBERS

1 Put these car prices in order, starting with the smallest.

£13 416   £14 316   £31 614
       £11 346   £13 146

| £ | £ | £ | £ | £ |

1 mark

2 Put these masses in order, starting with the heaviest.

5·05 kg   55·0 kg   5·0 kg   0·55 kg   5·5 kg

| kg | kg | kg | kg | kg |

1 mark

3 Find and mark the position of the following numbers on the number line.

3·8   3·95   4·2   3·75

3·7   4·0   4·3

2 marks

4 Put the < sign or the > sign in each box to make these number sentences correct.

(a) 135 cm [   ] 153 cm   (b) 1076 ml [   ] 1067 ml

(c) 0·03 [   ] 0·3

3 marks

5 Write a number which comes **between**:

(a) 63 and 78   [   ]

(b) 5·6 and 5·7   [   ]

(c) 9998 and 10 005   [   ]

3 marks

TOTAL [   ]

How did you score?

6 or less – try again!
7 or 8 – nearly there!
9 or 10 – well done!

ROUNDING NUMBERS

What you need to know

1 Round whole numbers to the nearest 10, 100 or 1000.

2 Round decimal numbers to the nearest unit or tenth (1 decimal place).

3 Use rounded numbers to estimate answers to calculations.

ROUNDING WHOLE NUMBERS

- To round whole numbers, look at the **digit** after the digit to which the number is to be **rounded**.
  If it is 4 or less, the number is rounded down.
  If it is 5 or more, it is rounded up.

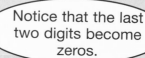

Notice that the last two digits become zeros.

Example   Round 3586 to the nearest hundred.

$$3586 \rightarrow 3600$$

This is the **hundreds** digit. Look at the **tens** digit to decide how to round.
It is 8, so round the hundreds digit up to 6.
The rounded number is written as 3600.

ROUNDING DECIMAL NUMBERS

- Decimal numbers may be rounded to one decimal place: tenths.

Example   Round 8·737 to the nearest tenth, or to one decimal place.
In 8·737, the tenths digit is 7.
Look at the hundredths digit. It is only 3, so the tenths digit is left as 7.
The rounded number is written as 8·7.

ESTIMATING ANSWERS

- It is often useful to **estimate** an answer to a **calculation** before working it out exactly. It gives you a rough idea about how big your answer should be. Sometimes an **approximate** answer is all that is needed.

Example   Imagine that you have £40 to spend on a new camera, a pair of binoculars and a notebook. You see them in a shop window but you're not sure if you will have enough money to pay for them all.

£3·89
£13·20
£21·75

You could round the prices to the nearest pound to estimate the total as £39. Now you know you have enough to buy all three items!

£13
£4

£22

ROUNDING NUMBERS

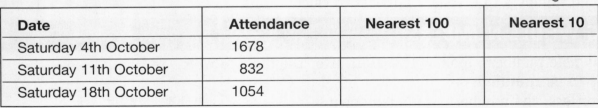

GOAL!

1 Kerry's local football team is Barnstone Rovers.
The numbers of people attending the team's last
three games are listed in the table below.

Round each of these numbers:
(a) to the nearest hundred   (b) to the nearest ten.

Date	Attendance	Nearest 100	Nearest 10
Saturday 4th October	1678		
Saturday 11th October	832		
Saturday 18th October	1054		

3 marks

2 Circle the number below that is nearest in value to 630.

599   699   701   656   530   600

1 mark

3 (a) Round all the decimals below to one decimal place.

0·45   0·62   0·51   0·89   0·09

☐   ☐   ☐   ☐   ☐

(b) Circle any decimals above which will round to 1 as their nearest
whole number.

2 marks

4 Put a tick next to any of these calculations that you think will work out to
approximately 200.

136 + 80 ☐   19 x 9 ☐   20 x 40 ☐   315 – 158 ☐

2 marks

5 There are 28 pupils in Class 6. The teacher is organizing a trip to the
museum for the class. Each pupil must pay £1.32 for the coach and £3.55
for the entrance fee for the museum.

Becky estimates that the total cost will be about £150.

Is she correct?   Circle   **Yes**   or   **No**.

Show how she could have estimated this.

2 marks

TOTAL ☐

TRIANGLES AND POLYGONS

What you need to know

1. Name, make, describe and classify triangles and polygons based on their properties.

2. Recognize equal sides, equal angles and right angles in triangles and polygons.

TYPES OF TRIANGLE

- There are 4 types of **triangle**: right-angled, equilateral, isosceles and scalene.

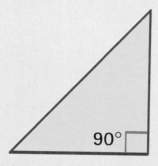

90°

right-angled triangle:
one 90 degree angle

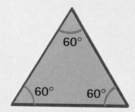

60°
60°   60°

equilateral triangle:
all **sides** the same length
all **angles** equal, each 60 degrees

isosceles triangle:
two sides the same length
two angles the same size

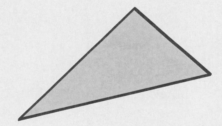

scalene triangle:
no sides the same length
no angles the same size

POLYGONS

- **Polygons** have straight sides.

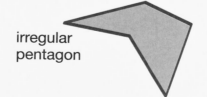

regular
pentagon

irregular
pentagon

Regular polygons have
sides of equal length.

Irregular polygons have
sides of different lengths.

Remember
A pentagon has 5 sides,
a hexagon has 6 sides,
a heptagon has 7 sides,
and an octagon has 8 sides.

pentagon   hexagon

heptagon   octagon

11

TRIANGLES AND POLYGONS

1 Look at these triangles.

Put an **E** inside the equilateral triangle,
an **I** inside the isosceles triangle, and
an **R** inside the right-angled triangle.

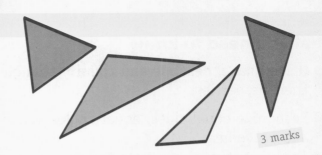

3 marks

2 Put a tick next to the statements which are true.

An isosceles triangle has
3 equal sides. ☐

An isosceles triangle has
2 equal angles. ☐

A scalene triangle has
no equal sides. ☐

An equilateral triangle has
one pair of parallel sides. ☐

2 marks

3 Brian has made a chart to classify shapes.
He has not finished filling it in.
Look at the shapes and their properties
and help Brian to complete his chart.

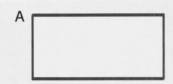
A

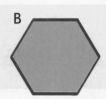
B

C

D

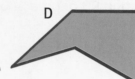

Put a tick if the statement is true or a
cross if it is false.

Shape	Parallel sides	All sides of equal length	Has at least one right angle
A		✗	✓
B	✓		✗
C			✗
D	✗		

3 marks

4 On the grid below draw a **pentagon** which has **three right angles**.

2 marks

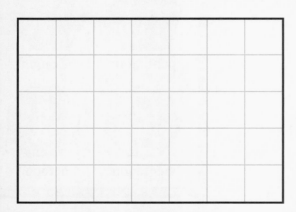

TOTAL ☐

How did
you score?

6 or less – try again!
7 or 8 – nearly there!
9 or 10 – well done!

QUADRILATERALS

What you need to know

1 Know that all four-sided shapes are quadrilaterals.

2 Recognize the common quadrilaterals: square, rectangle, rhombus, parallelogram, trapezium and kite.

3 Name, describe, make and classify quadrilaterals.

COMMON QUADRILATERALS

Remember
Quadrilaterals are four-sided shapes. Quadrilateral means four-sided.

- Some quadrilaterals have special names, such as: **square**, **rectangle**, **rhombus**, **parallelogram**, **trapezium** and **kite**.

- Quadrilaterals can be classified according to their properties:
equal sides   number of **right angles**   pairs of **parallel** lines.

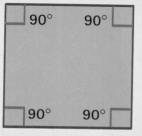

square:
all sides the same length
four right angles

rectangle:
two pairs of equal sides
four right angles

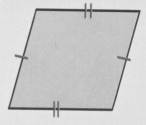

rhombus:
all sides the same length
opposite sides are parallel
opposite angles are the same size

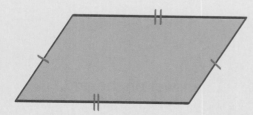

parallelogram:
two pairs of equal sides
opposite sides are parallel
opposite angles are the same size

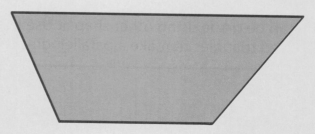

trapezium:
one pair of parallel sides

What am I?
I have four sides.
I have two pairs of equal sides.
I do not have any parallel sides.
What am I?

two pairs of equal, adjacent sides

What is the difference between a square and a rhombus?
They both have 4 equal sides and 2 pairs of parallel sides, **but** the angles in a square are all 90°. In a rhombus the angles are **not** 90°.

Answer: kite

QUADRILATERALS

1 Look at the quadrilaterals below. Name each quadrilateral and mark any pairs of parallel lines.

3 marks

_____   _____   _____

2 (a) Draw a quadrilateral with 4 right angles and 2 pairs of parallel sides.

1 mark

(b) Draw a quadrilateral with no right angles.

1 mark

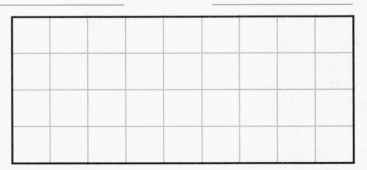

3 Put a tick inside the shapes that are quadrilaterals.

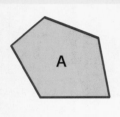  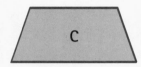 

A   B   C   D   E

3 marks

4 Draw a line inside this regular hexagon to divide it into 2 trapeziums.

1 mark

5 Shapes can be made using other shapes. Use these two right-angled triangles to make a parallelogram.

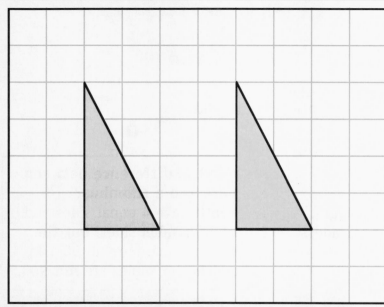

Draw your answer on the grid.

1 mark

TOTAL [   ]

ADDITION CALCULATIONS

What you need to know

1 Use written methods for adding whole numbers and decimals.

2 Check answers using a different method or by estimating first.

3 Recognize that addition is the inverse of subtraction.

4 Work out word problems which use addition.

> Look for **doubles** or near doubles, or numbers which **add** up to 1, 10 or 100 and add them first.

ADDING NUMBERS UNDER 100

• The best method to choose for adding numbers together will depend very much on the numbers given in the question or problem.

Example   To add the numbers 35 and 37, a mental method would probably be best.

Either   **double** 35 to give 70, then **add** the extra 2 (from the 37) to get 72.
Or   add 30 and 30 to get 60, then add 5 and 7 to get 12.
          Now add 60 and 12 to get 72.

ADDING HIGHER NUMBERS

• To add higher numbers, such as 138 and 56, use a written method.

Example   Start at 138 and **count on** 50 to get to 188,
           now from 188, count on 6 to get 194.

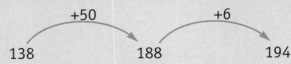

    +50   +6

  138   188   194

Or   first calculate 130 + 50   = 180
      then calculate 8 + 6   =   14 +
                                      194

Or   use a formal column method

$$\begin{array}{r} 138 \\ {}_156+ \\ \hline 194 \end{array}$$

Quick Tips!

• Read problems carefully.
• **Total**, **sum** and **altogether** indicate an addition calculation.
• Estimate your answer first and check your addition using a different method.

USING SUBTRACTION

• Subtraction can be used to solve some addition problems where you know the answer and are trying to find one of the numbers.

Example   45 + ☐ = 87
           This means: 'what must be added to 45 to make 87?'
           Think of this calculation as a subtraction instead, 87 − 45 = 42
           Check the answer by adding 45 and 42.
           The total is 87, so 42 is the correct answer!

> **Remember**
> **Addition** is the **inverse** of subtraction.

ADDITION CALCULATIONS

1 Calculate:

(a)   16 + 17 + 18

(b)   345 + 279

(c)   15·5 + 0·96

3 marks

2 Write the missing numbers in each number sentence.

(a)   92 + ☐ = 113

(b)   6 ☐ + ☐ 4 = 100

(c)   200 − ☐ = 58

3 marks

3 Circle a pair of numbers which give a total of 100.

    43   86   39   57   15   61

1 mark

4 Write in the missing numbers so that each
side of the triangle has a total of 1.

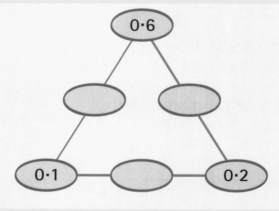

1 mark

5 Use the digits **4**, **6**, **7** and **9** to complete the addition calculation.

```
  ☐  3  ☐
  4  ☐  7  +
 ─────────
  ☐  1  3
```

2 marks

TOTAL ☐

SUBTRACTION CALCULATIONS

What you need to know

1 Use written methods for subtracting whole numbers and decimals.

2 Check answers using a different method or by estimating first.

3 Recognize that subtraction is the inverse of addition.

4 Work out word problems which use subtraction.

SUBTRACTING WHOLE NUMBERS

- The best method to choose for subtracting two numbers will depend very much on the numbers given in the question or problem.

Example   To find the **difference** between 49 and 18, a mental method would probably be best.

Either   round 49 to 50 first, then calculate 50 – 18 = 32.
Now **take off** 1 (because 50 is one more than 49) to give 31.

Or   **count on** from 18 to 49.

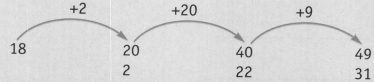

Add 31 to get from 18 to 49, so 49 – 18 = 31.

> **Remember**
> - Subtraction is the inverse of addition.
> - In a subtraction calculation, the answer will be less than the largest number you started with.
> - Answers to subtraction calculations may be checked using addition.

SUBTRACTING DECIMAL NUMBERS

- To subtract two decimal numbers, such as $0 \cdot 7 - 0 \cdot 32$, one way could be as follows:

Write as $0 \cdot 70 - 0 \cdot 32$
then calculate 70 – 32 = 38
rewrite the answer as a decimal $0 \cdot 38$.
Check the answer by adding: $0 \cdot 32 + 0 \cdot 38 = 0 \cdot 70$.

SUBTRACTING HIGHER NUMBERS

- To **subtract** higher numbers, such as 375 and 187, and for harder decimal numbers, such as $1 \cdot 63 - 0 \cdot 9$, a written method may be more sensible.

Example

$$
\begin{array}{r}
3\overset{2\;\overset{1}{6}\;1}{7}5 \\
187\;- \\
\hline
188
\end{array}
$$

$$
\begin{array}{r}
\overset{0\;\;1}{1}.63 \\
0.90\;- \\
\hline
0.73
\end{array}
$$

These are formal methods of setting out.

Be careful!

Some questions may look like additions but you need to use subtraction to work out the answer.

Example $35 + \square = 58$.

Work it out by calculating 58 — 35.

SUBTRACTION CALCULATIONS

1 Write in the missing numbers or digits to make these calculations correct.

(a) $200 -$ ☐ $= 134$ (b) 87 ☐ $-$ ☐ $54 = 617$

2 marks

2 Circle the pair of numbers with the greater difference.

$123 - 45$ $129 - 56$

1 mark

3 Liam and Polly both collect stamps.

52p   37p   19p   5p   2p   1p

(a) Liam has 500 stamps and gives 138 of them to Polly.
How many does Liam have left?

1 mark

(b) Polly now has 247 stamps.
How many did she have before Liam gave her some of his stamps?

1 mark

4 Calculate $1807 - 769$.

1 mark

5 179 passengers board an empty train.
38 passengers get off the train at the first station.
54 passengers get off the train at the second station.

How many passengers are left on the train after the second stop?

1 mark

6 Kerry is thinking of two positive numbers.
Both of the numbers are less than 20.
The two numbers have a difference of 17.

Write all the possible pairs of numbers she could be thinking of.

2 marks

7 Complete the number statement.

$3·6 -$ ☐ $= 4·7 - 2·9$

1 mark

How did
you score?

TOTAL ☐

6 or less – try again!
7 or 8 – nearly there!
9 or 10 – well done!

18

SYMMETRY IN 2-D SHAPES

What you need to know

1 Draw lines of symmetry on a range of 2-D shapes.

2 Understand that a symmetrical shape is exactly the same on both sides of the line of symmetry.

2-D SHAPES

- If a line can be drawn through a 2-D shape so that the shape on either side of the line looks exactly the same, it is called a **line of symmetry**. The shape is said to have **reflective symmetry**.

Quick Tip!

You can check for lines of symmetry by tracing a shape and folding it, or by using a mirror.

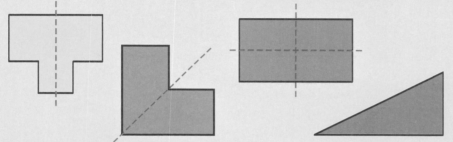

Some shapes have just one line of symmetry while some shapes have more than one.

Lines of symmetry can be **diagonal** as well as **vertical** and **horizontal**.

Some shapes have no lines of symmetry at all.

Remember
- A shape may have more than one line of symmetry.
- A rectangle has 2 lines of symmetry, **not** 4.
- A parallelogram has **no** lines of symmetry.

REGULAR POLYGONS

- A regular polygon (a many-sided shape) has as many lines of symmetry as it has sides.

  A regular pentagon has five lines of symmetry, a regular hexagon has six.

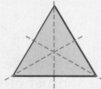 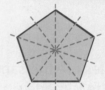 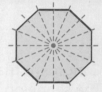

equilateral triangle   regular pentagon   regular octagon

DIFFERENT LINES OF SYMMETRY

- A shape can be made to have different lines of symmetry by adding extra parts to it.

Example   Look at the first shape below. More squares can be added to make it into a shape with different lines of symmetry:

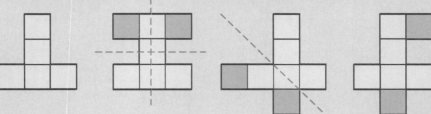

SYMMETRY IN 2-D SHAPES

1 Draw in all the lines of symmetry you can see in these shapes.

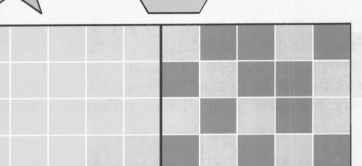

A

B

C

3 marks

2 Complete the pattern so it is symmetrical about the straight black line.

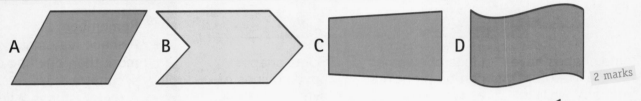

1 mark

3 Put a tick inside the shapes below that have reflective symmetry.

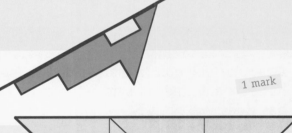

A   B   C   D

2 marks

4 Complete the shape on the right which has reflective symmetry about the straight black line.

1 mark

5 Congruent triangles are the same shape and size. The shape opposite is made up of 4 congruent triangles.

Draw 2 more triangles to make each complete shape have:

(a)   1 line of symmetry   (b)   2 lines of symmetry   (c)   0 lines of symmetry.

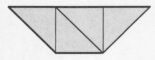   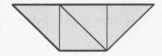   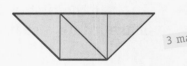

3 marks

How did you score?

TOTAL

6 or less – try again!
7 or 8 – nearly there!
9 or 10 – well done!

3-D SHAPES

What you need to know

1. Name, make, describe and classify 3-D shapes based on their properties.
2. Identify different nets of 3-D shapes.
3. Visualize 3-D shapes from 3-D drawings.

FLAT FACES

- These 3-D shapes all have flat faces.

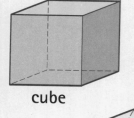
cube

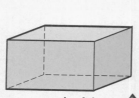
cuboid

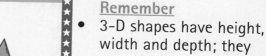
triangular-based pyramid

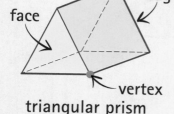
face   edge   vertex
triangular prism

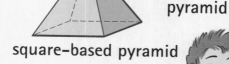
square-based pyramid

Remember
- 3-D shapes have height, width and depth; they are solid shapes.
- 3-D shapes have **edges**, **faces** and **vertices**.
- A **vertex** is a point at which edges meet; it is another word for corner.
- Vertices is the plural of vertex.

Prisms have faces of the same shape at both ends.

CURVED FACES

- Some shapes, such as **cones**, **spheres** and **cylinders**, have curved faces.

cone

cylinder

sphere

NETS

- If you unfolded a 3-D shape and drew round the outline, the resulting shape on the paper would be its **net**.
- For some 3-D shapes there may be more than one possible net.

Example   Two of several possible nets for a cuboid are:

Quick Tip!

The best way to learn about nets is to cut up some different-shaped cardboard boxes and investigate them yourself. Try drawing some nets and check they work by cutting and folding them.

3-D SHAPES

1 Claire and Sean have been looking at 3-D shapes.
They have been counting the edges, faces and vertices.

Complete the table.

Shape		Faces	Edges	Vertices
cuboid			12	
triangular prism				6
square-based pyramid			8	

6 marks

2 Here are some nets. Some of them will fold to make up a square-based pyramid and some will not.

Tick the nets that will form a complete shape and put a cross inside those that will not.

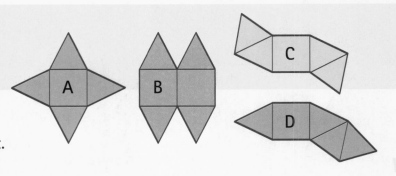

2 marks

3 Kieran has made a paper cone.

Put a tick inside the piece of paper which, when folded, makes a cone.

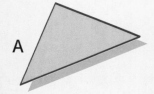 A   B    C   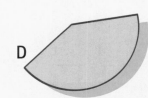 D

1 mark

4 Barry has made a cylinder out of clay.
He uses a knife to cut the cylinder in half as shown.

Sketch the shape of the cut face below.

1 mark

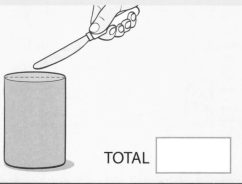

TOTAL

USING A CALCULATOR

What you need to know

1 Know how to use a calculator correctly.

2 Use a calculator to check estimated or written calculations.

3 Use a calculator to interpret money calculations.

4 Change a fraction into a decimal using a calculator.

5 Recognize decimal fractions on a calculator display.

TWO-PART CALCULATIONS

- For more difficult calculations you may need to do them in more than one step.

Example
To **calculate** $(13 \cdot 5 + 1 \cdot 6)$ x $(5 \cdot 6 - 1 \cdot 2)$,
first work out $13 \cdot 5 + 1 \cdot 6$ and write your answer down,
then work out $5 \cdot 6 - 1 \cdot 2$ and write your answer down,
now multiply these two answers together.

> ### Quick Tip!
>
> Check answers worked out on a calculator by using an inverse calculation, or by estimating an approximate answer before you start.

MONEY CALCULATIONS

- When working with money problems, be careful to read the **display** correctly.

Example
To work out the cost of 15 pencils costing 48p,
15 x $0 \cdot 48$ on the calculator gives the answer $7 \cdot 2$.
Remember to read this as £7.20.

FRACTIONS TO DECIMALS

- A fraction can be changed to a decimal by dividing the **numerator** (top number) by the **denominator** (bottom number).

$$\tfrac{3}{8} \rightarrow 3 \div 8 \rightarrow 0 \cdot 375.$$

Save time!
- A calculator is useful for solving problems which would otherwise take a long time to work out using a written method.

Example
To find the two consecutive numbers which multiply to give 552, you could start by choosing any two consecutive numbers, say 20 and 21.

20 x 21 = 420   too small so try two larger numbers
25 x 26 = 650   too large so try two numbers in between
23 x 24 = 552   correct!

USING A CALCULATOR

1 Use your calculator to work out

77·84 ÷ 5·6 = ⬚

1 mark

2 Rebecca is 150 cm tall and Natalie is 173 cm tall. Stefanie's height is exactly halfway between Rebecca's and Natalie's heights.

How tall is Stefanie?

⬚ cm

1 mark

3 At a school play, 326 tickets were sold. Each ticket cost 55p.

How much money was raised altogether?

⬚

1 mark

4 Change these fractions into decimal numbers.

(a) $\frac{4}{5}$ (b) $\frac{2}{3}$ (c) $\frac{5}{8}$

⬚   ⬚   ⬚

3 marks

5 Calculate the length of each side of a square room, if the area of the room is 169 m².

⬚ m

1 mark

6 Write the missing number in this calculation.

846·3 ÷ ⬚ = 120·9

1 mark

7 Use a calculator to work out the answer to this calculation.

(39 + 16) x (45 – 29) = ⬚

1 mark

8 The same number is missing from each box.

Write the missing number in each box.

⬚ x ⬚ x ⬚ = 2197

1 mark

TOTAL ⬚

How did you score?

6 or less – try again!
7 or 8 – nearly there!
9 or 10 – well done!

MULTIPLICATION CALCULATIONS

What you need to know

1 Recall multiplication facts (times tables).

2 Use different mental methods to multiply whole numbers and simple decimal numbers.

3 Use a suitable written method for multiplying whole and decimal numbers by one- and two-digit numbers.

Remember
Multiplication is the inverse of division:
if 3 x 9 = 27
then 27 ÷ 9 = 3.

MENTAL METHODS

- The best method to choose for multiplying two numbers together will depend very much on the numbers given in the question or problem.

Examples

6 x 9   Recall your **multiplication** (tables) facts to get 54.

14 x 7   **Either** calculate 7 x 7 = 49, then double this to get 98.
Or calculate 10 x 7 = 70 and 4 x 7 = 28,
then add these two answers to give 98.

23 x 15   **Either** calculate 23 x 10 = 230,
then halve this 23 x 5 = 115,
now add these two answers to give 345.
Or calculate 23 x 30 = 690,
then halve it to get 345.

0·6 x 4   Calculate 6 x 4 = 24,
then 'add' the decimal point to give 2·4.

Quick Tip!

Some multiplication facts can be used to find other multiplication and division facts.
Use 38 x 7 = 266
to give 266 ÷ 7 = 38
38 x 70 = 2660
3·8 x 7 = 26·6

WRITTEN METHODS

- For more difficult numbers a written method is probably best.

Examples   37 x 184

```
  2 5 1 2
    1 8 4
     3 7 x
  1 2 8 8
  5,5 2 0 +
  6 8 0 8
```

Or

×	100	80	4		
30	3000	2400	120	5520	5 5 2 0
7	700	560	28	1288	1 2 8 8 +
					6 8 0 8

Or

```
  1 8 4          1 8 4
      7 x            3 x
  1 2 8 8          5 5 2     then x 10 = 5520
```

25

MULTIPLICATION CALCULATIONS

1 Write the missing numbers.

4 x 12 = ☐ ☐ x 7 = 63

2 marks

2 What number when multiplied by 7 makes 35? ☐

1 mark

3 Look at this multiplication: 6 x 4.

Find two more numbers which multiply together to give the same product.
Write your numbers in the boxes below.

☐ x ☐

1 mark

4 Complete the multiplication grid.

One square in the grid has been completed for you.

×	5	3
6	30	
5		

1 mark

5 A chef uses four boxes of eggs to make a large quantity of fresh custard.
Eggs are packed in boxes of six.

How many eggs does the chef use to make the custard? ☐

1 mark

6 A football club has booked 7 coaches to take supporters to a cup match.
Each coach can seat 52 passengers.

How many supporters can travel on the coaches provided? ☐

1 mark

7 Calculate 523 x 21.

Show your working. ☐

2 marks

8 Shaun knows that 36 x 18 = 648.

Explain how he can write the answer to 18 x 18 without working out the multiplication.

1 mark

TOTAL ☐

How did you score?

6 or less – try again!
7 or 8 – nearly there!
9 or 10 – well done!

PROPERTIES OF NUMBERS

What you need to know

1 Recognize odd and even numbers.

2 Recognize and find factors or multiples of a number, or numbers.

3 Know that a prime number has only two factors and know the prime numbers to at least 30.

4 Recognize and find square numbers and square roots in terms of 'the number multiplied by itself'.

ODD AND EVEN NUMBERS

- **Even** numbers end in 0, 2, 4, 6 or 8
- All even numbers are **divisible** by 2.
- **Odd** numbers end in 1, 3, 5, 7 or 9

32   1800

75   40303

> **Remember**
> Some numbers can have several properties.
> 5 is an odd number
>   a prime number
>   a multiple of 5
>   a factor of 30

FACTORS AND MULTIPLES

- **Factors** are numbers that divide exactly into a number.

   factors of 8: 1, 2, 4 and 8

- **Multiples** of a number are the answers to the tables of that number.

   multiples of 7: 7, 14, 21, 28, 35, …

- A good way to find all the factors of a number is to think of all the pairs of numbers which **multiply** to give that number.

   factors of 30: 1 x 30   2 x 15   3 x 10   5 x 6
   so the factors of 30 are: 1, 2, 3, 5, 6, 10, 15 and 30

PRIME NUMBERS

- A **prime** number has only two factors: 1 and the number itself.

   23 only has factors 1 and 23

- The first few prime numbers are 2, 3, 5, 7, 11, 13, 17, 19, 23, 29.

SQUARE NUMBERS

- A **square number** is found by multiplying a number by itself.

   1 squared, or $1^2 = 1 \times 1 = 1$; $2^2 = 2 \times 2 = 4$; $3^2 = 3 \times 3 = 9$

- The square root of a number can be thought of as the number you must multiply by itself to get a **square number**.

   The square root of 25 is 5, (since 5 x 5 = 25).

Quick Tip!

Numbers which are divisible by:
5   end in 0 or 5
3   have digits which add up to a number which is divisible by 3
9   have digits which add up to a number which is divisible by 9
4   have the last 2 digits which are divisible by 4.

PROPERTIES OF NUMBERS

1 Complete this three-digit number so that it is a multiple of 7.

3		

1 mark

2 Circle the numbers that are prime numbers.

9 7 13 16 27

1 mark

3 Write down a two-digit even number that is also a square number.

1 mark

4 Write down a number that has the factors 5 and 6.

1 mark

5 A bakery makes 12 852 jam tarts in one day. The tarts are packed into boxes of three.

(a) Without dividing the number of tarts by 3, explain how it is possible to say that there will be no tarts left over after packing.

1 mark

(b) The bakery decides to pack the tarts into boxes of four. Explain how you can check whether there will be any tarts left over after packing.

1 mark

6 Harpreet and Joe count aloud together from 1 to 30.
Harpreet bangs a drum on every third number.
Joe rings a bell on every fifth number.

How many times will the drum and bell sound together?

1 mark

7 Look at the list of numbers. Circle all the numbers which are factors of 30.

4 15 7 3 10 12

2 marks

8 Stevie says, 'I am thinking of a number. My number is between 1 and 25, it is a multiple of 7 and also a multiple of 3'.

What is Stevie's number?

1 mark

TOTAL

How did you score?

6 or less – try again!
7 or 8 – nearly there!
9 or 10 – well done!

NUMBER SEQUENCES

What you need to know

1 Describe the rule linking numbers in a sequence.

2 Create, complete or extend a number sequence using a given rule and predict further terms.

3 Describe and extend sequences of patterns.

4 Recognize sequences of odd numbers, even numbers, square numbers and multiples.

FIND THE RULE

- A **sequence** is a list of numbers that are linked by a **rule**. If you know or can work out the rule, you can find the next numbers in the sequence.

Example

Here are some **number sequences**.

–9   –1   7   15   23

The next number is found by adding on 8.

4   8   12   16   20

The next number is found by adding on 4.
These numbers are also the **multiples** of 4.

640 320 160 80   40

The next number is found by dividing by two, or halving.

The sequence of square numbers starts 1, 4, 9, 16, 25, 36, 49, 64 ...

- To find numbers at the start of the sequence you will need to work backwards by doing the inverse of the rule.

Example

Find the first two numbers in this sequence.

☐ ☐ 19   27   35   43

The rule is add 8 but to get the first two numbers you will need to subtract 8 and work backwards to complete the sequence.

3   11   19   27   35   43

PATTERNS

- Some sequences can be shown as **patterns**.

3

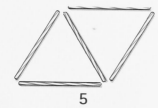
5

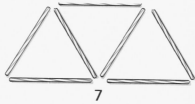
7

The next pattern is found by adding two more straws. Nine straws would be needed to make the fourth pattern.

This sequence of patterns uses a different number of straws each time.
The number of straws makes the sequence 3, 5, 7 ...

NUMBER SEQUENCES

1 Fill in the missing numbers in the sequence.

37   29   ☐   13   ☐

1 mark

Explain the rule for the sequence.

_____

1 mark

2 Jenna makes pendants of different sizes. She uses rubies (●) and diamonds (◊) to make the designs.

Size 1   Size 2   Size 3

(a)   How many rubies will Jenna need to make a size 6 pendant?   ☐

1 mark

(b)   How many rubies will a pendant with 16 diamonds have?   ☐

1 mark

3 The first five multiples of 35 are listed as a sequence below.

35   70   105   140   175

Henry says, 'If the sequence is continued, the twelfth number will be 425'.
Without working out the twelfth number, explain why Henry is wrong.

_____

1 mark

4 Jodie is making number sequences. In one sequence, she starts with the number 3 and makes the next number in the sequence by doubling it and adding 1.

Write down the next three numbers in her sequence.

3   ☐   ☐   ☐

3 marks

5 Fill in the missing numbers in this number sequence.

5   10   15   20   ☐
   9   14   ☐   24

1 mark

Explain the rule that you have used to find the missing numbers.

1 mark

_____

TOTAL   ☐

How did you score?

6 or less – try again!
7 or 8 – nearly there!
9 or 10 – well done!

ANGLES

What you need to know

1 Know that angles are measured in degrees and that one whole turn is 360°.

2 Recognize acute, right, obtuse and reflex angles.

3 Estimate, measure, draw and compare angles.

4 Know and use simple angle facts.

ANGLE FACTS

- An angle is a measure of turn.
- Angles are measured in **degrees**.
- One whole turn is 360°.
- One quarter turn is 90°, or a **right angle**.

An angle less than 90° is **acute**.

An angle between 90° and 180° is **obtuse**.

An angle greater than 180° is **reflex**.

110° 70°

Angles in a straight line add up to 180°.

Angles at a point add up to 360°.

80°
140° 140°

In the special case of an **equilateral** triangle, each angle is 60°.

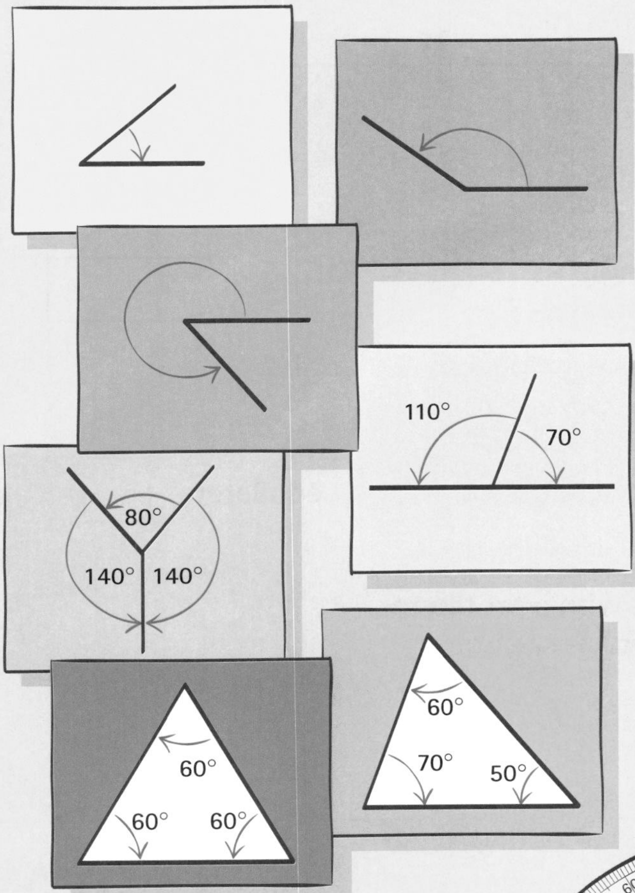

60°
60° 60°

60°
70° 50°

Angles inside a triangle add up to 180°.

Always measure round from 0 when measuring an angle with a protractor.

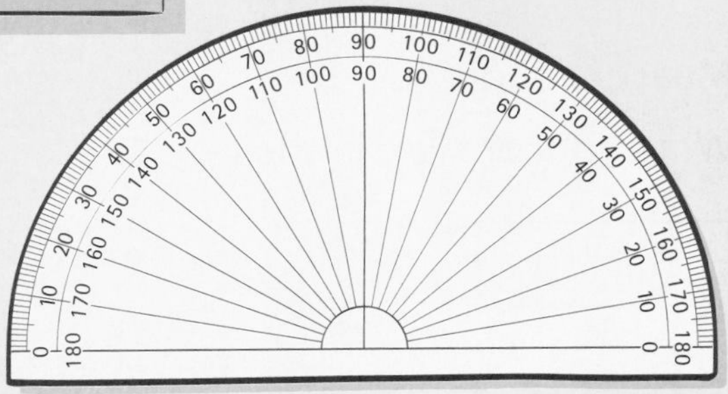

1 Complete the table.

number of right angles	$\frac{1}{2}$	1	$1\frac{1}{2}$			4
degrees		90°		180°	270°	

3 marks

2 Look at the angle below.

For each sentence, put a tick if it is true or a cross if it is false.

(a) The angle is an obtuse angle. ☐   (b) The angle is less than a right angle. ☐

(c) The angle is greater than 45°. ☐   (d) The angle is an acute angle. ☐   2 marks

3 Here is a piece of wallpaper border.

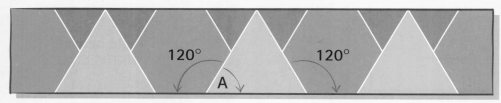

120°   120°

A

(a) Work out the size of angle A.
Do not *use a protractor to measure it.*   ☐ °   1 mark

(b) What type of triangle is each pale pink triangle?   1 mark

Put a tick in the correct box.

isosceles ☐   right angled ☐   equilateral ☐   scalene ☐

4 Asim cut out a triangle from a piece of paper. He measured two of the angles with a protractor. He did not measure the third angle but said that it must be 38°.

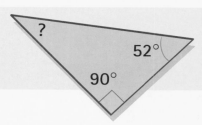

?   52°   90°

Explain why Asim is correct.

_____

2 marks

5 Measure angle A.

Write your answer in the box.

☐

1 mark

A

TOTAL ☐

PROBABILITY

What you need to know

1 Work out probabilities of events with two or more equally likely outcomes.

2 Place events on a probability scale.

3 Start to understand that the results of an experiment can give different probabilities to those calculated.

PROBABILITY IN WORDS

- **Probability** is a measure of how **likely** it is for something to happen.

  It is **very unlikely** that it will snow in July.
  The probability of getting a 6 on a dice is $\frac{1}{6}$.
  However, if you roll a dice six times it does not necessarily follow that you will get one 6.

- For many everyday events there is usually more than one **outcome**.

  A football team may win, draw or lose their next match.

- Some events have **equally likely** outcomes, e.g. tossing a coin.

Example

You have 4 white counters in a bag.
You also have some black counters.
How many black counters would you need to put in the bag
(a) for there to be an **even chance** of picking a black or white counter? The answer is 4.
(b) to make it **more likely** to pick a black counter than a white counter? The answer is 5 or more.

USING NUMBERS

- All probabilities lie between 0 (impossible) and 1 (certain).
- Probabilities are usually written as fractions.

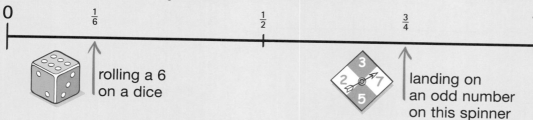

0          $\frac{1}{6}$ $\frac{1}{2}$ $\frac{3}{4}$ 1

rolling a 6 on a dice

landing on an odd number on this spinner

SNEAKY SPINNER!
Which number is the spinner more likely to land on?
The answer is neither! There is an even chance of landing on 1 or 2.
Remember that it is the angle which the pointer turns through that matters.
Through one half turn it will land on 1 and in the next half turn it will land on 2.

PROBABILITY

1 This spinner can land on the numbers 1, 2, or 3.

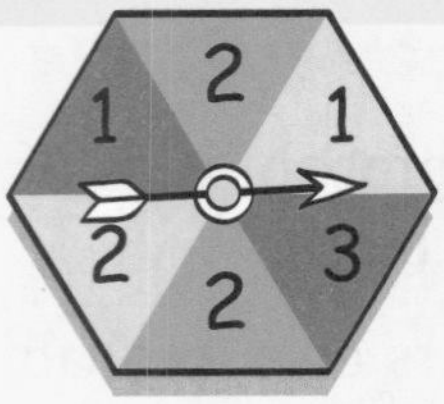

(a) What is the probability of the spinner landing on 3?

1 mark

(b) Which number is the spinner most likely to land on?
Give a reason.

1 mark

1 mark

---

2 A bag contains 10 green balls. How many white balls must be added to the bag so that there is an even chance of taking a green ball out at random?

1 mark

---

3 Hassan is making a spinner to use in a game.
He has marked some numbers on it as shown here.

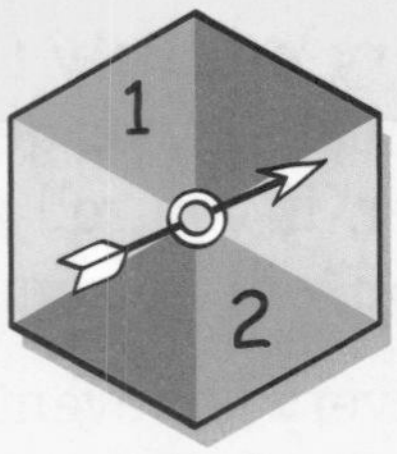

(a) Using only the numbers 1 and 2, write numbers in the empty parts of the spinner so that there is more chance of landing on 2 than 1.

2 marks

(b) Hassan has made another spinner.
Hassan thinks that there is more chance of spinning a 2 than a 1.
Is he correct?
Circle **Yes** or **No**.
Explain why.

1 mark

1 mark

---

4 Gary has two bags of counters.
The probability of selecting a black counter from bag A is $\frac{3}{10}$. The arrow marked A shows this probability on the probability scale.

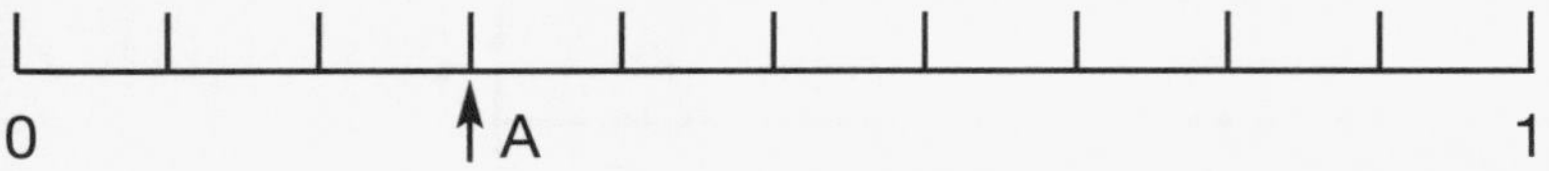

0   ↑A   1

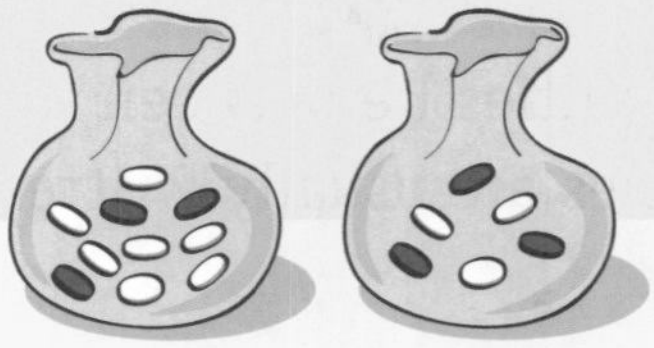

(a) Mark an arrow to show the probability of selecting a black counter from bag B.

1 mark

(b) How many black counters should be added to bag C so that the probability of picking a black counter is $\frac{2}{5}$?

C

1 mark

TOTAL

How did you score?

6 or less – try again!
7 or 8 – nearly there!
9 or 10 – well done!

DIVISION CALCULATIONS

What you need to know

1 Use multiplication facts to help recall division facts.

2 Use different mental methods to divide whole numbers and simple decimal numbers.

3 Use a suitable written method for dividing whole and decimal numbers by one- and two-digit numbers.

MENTAL METHODS

- The best method to choose for dividing one number by another will depend very much on the numbers given in the question or problem.

Examples	
$16 \div 4$	Recall your division facts to get 4 (or use the fact that $4 \times 4 = 16$).
$28 \div 5$	Recall the division fact of $25 \div 5 = 5$, then count on 3 to 28, giving the answer 5 remainder 3.
$364 \div 2$	Halve 364 by first halving 300 to get 150, then halving 64 to get 32, giving the answer 182.
$3 \cdot 5 \div 7$	Calculate $35 \div 7$ to get 5, then make the answer 10 times smaller to give $0 \cdot 5$, since $3 \cdot 5$ is ten times smaller than 35.
$96 \div 16$	Calculate this as two divisions, first by 2, then by 8 (since $2 \times 8 = 16$): $96 \div 2 = 48$, then $48 \div 8 = 6$.

> **Remember**
> Division is the inverse of multiplication.
> If $40 \div 5 = 8$
> then $8 \times 5 = 40$

WRITTEN METHODS

- For more difficult numbers a written method is probably best.

Examples $313 \div 18$

```
            1 7 r 7
   18) 3 1 3
      - 1 8            1 8
        1 3 3            7 x
      - 1 2 6          1 2 6
            7
Or      3 1 3
      - 1 8 0      10  x 18 (180)
        1 3 3
      -   9 0       5  x  18 (90)
          4 3
      -   3 6       2  x  18 (36)
remainder   7      17  lots of  18      so the answer is 17 r 7
```

Quick Tip!

You can use a multiplication fact to find division facts.
If $54 \times 13 = 702$
then $702 \div 54 = 13$
         $702 \div 5 \cdot 4 = 130$

DIVISION CALCULATIONS

1 Circle the division questions which have the answer 6.

$14 \div 2$ $24 \div 4$ $27 \div 3$ $32 \div 4$ $30 \div 5$

1 mark

2 Write the missing number.

$44 \div$ [ ] $= 11$

1 mark

3 Jake writes a number on a card.
He asks Frances to guess the number on the card by giving her a clue.
He says, 'If I divide the number on the card by 4 it gives the answer 32.'

What is the number on the card? [ ]

1 mark

4 Calculate:

(a) $1267 \div 7 =$ [ ]   (b) $365 \div 24 =$ [ ]

2 marks

5 Look at this multiplication fact: $6 \times 27 = 162$.

Use this to write the answer to $162 \div 27 =$ [ ]

1 mark

6 Tony has made 58 toffee cakes for the
cake stall at the school fair. He decides to
put four cakes in a bag.

How many bags can he fill? [ ]

1 mark

7 Kylie's teacher has asked her to work out the answer to
$108 \div 18$.

Explain how Kylie can use the two division statements
below to work out the answer to the teacher's question.

$108 \div 2 = 54$ $54 \div 9 = 6$

1 mark

8 Year 6 are travelling to the museum in mini-buses.
There are 93 children in Year 6.
Each mini-bus can carry 14 children.

How many mini-buses will be needed? [ ]

1 mark

9 Write the missing number.

$48 \div$ [ ] $= 40 \div 5$ 1 mark   TOTAL [ ]

MULTIPLYING AND DIVIDING

What you need to know

1. Multiply and divide whole and decimal numbers by 10, 100 or 1000.

2. Multiply and divide multiples of 10, 100 or 1000 by a single digit number.

3. Multiply and divide multiples of 10, 100 or 1000 by other multiples of 10, 100 or 1000.

MULTIPLYING BY 10, 100 AND 1000

- To **multiply** a number by 10, move the digits 1 place to the left.
- To multiply by 100, move the digits 2 places to the left.
- To multiply by 1000, move the digits 3 places to the left.
- A **place value** chart is useful to see how multiplying a number by 10, 100 or 1000 changes the number.

Example

To calculate 35 x 1000, move all the digits three places to the left and add the zeros to give 35 000.

tens of thousands	thousands	hundreds	tens	units
			3	5
3	5	0	0	0

DIVIDING BY 10, 100 AND 1000

- To **divide** a number by 10, move the digits 1 place to the right.
- To divide by 100, move the digits 2 places to the right.
- To divide by 1000, move the digits 3 places to the right.
- You can use the same place value chart to divide a number by 10, 100 or 100.

Examples

To calculate 78 ÷ 100, move all the digits two places to the right to give 0·78.

tens of thousands	thousands	hundreds	tens	units	tenths	hundredths
			7	8		
				0	7	8

This method can be included in more difficult questions such as: 3 x 40.
Think of this as 3 x 4 x 10 = 12 x 10 = 120.

Or   600 ÷ 30
Think of this as 600 ÷ (10 x 3),
then work out 600 ÷ 10 = 60, then 60 ÷ 3 = 20.

MULTIPLYING AND DIVIDING

1 Write the missing numbers.

$9000 \div 100 = $ ⬚

$832 \times$ ⬚ $= 83\ 200$

$5·7 \times 10 = $ ⬚

⬚ $\div 10 = 0·8$

$40 \times 70 = $ ⬚

5 marks

2 What number is 10 times smaller than 32?

⬚

1 mark

3 How many times larger is 5600 than 56?

⬚

1 mark

4 Each day Donna delivers 53 newspapers on her paper round.

How many newspapers will she have delivered in 100 days?

⬚

1 mark

5 Kerry's uncle has 150 lettuce seeds which he wants to sow in his vegetable garden.
He has prepared 10 rows in which to plant the seeds.

How many seeds should he sow in each row?

⬚

1 mark

6 Heechan has asked each child in his school to bring in 20 tokens for the school's free books appeal.
There are 90 children in Heechan's school.

How many tokens can he expect to collect?

⬚

1 mark

TOTAL ⬚

UNITS AND THEIR CONVERSIONS

What you need to know

1 Know the relationships between metric units of length, mass and capacity.

2 Use the relationships between metric units to convert a measure from one unit to another.

3 Know the approximate metric equivalents of imperial units still in everyday use.

CONVERTING QUANTITIES

- It is very useful to be able to convert quantities into different units.

Example
> How many centimetres are there in 3 metres?
> Since 1 metre is 100 centimetres
> then 3 metres must be 300 centimetres.

- For more difficult cases it is useful to have a method to follow.

  Firstly, it is important to know the units in order of size.

  small ⟶ large

Length	mm ⟶ cm ⟶ m ⟶ km
Mass	g ⟶ kg ⟶ t
Capacity	ml ⟶ cl ⟶ l

  Secondly, you need to know the link between the two units you are using.

Imperial equivalents

Length: 8 kilometres is about 5 **miles**

Mass: 1 kilogram is about 2 **pounds (lb)**
30 grams is about 1 **ounce (oz)**

Capacity: 1 litre is about 2 **pints**
4·5 litres is about 1 **gallon**, or 8 pints

Metric units

Length:
1 **kilometre (km)** = 1000 **metres (m)**
1 metre = 1000 **millimetres (mm)**
1 metre = 100 **centimetres (cm)**
1 centimetre = 10 millimetres

Mass:
1 **tonne (t)** = 1000 **kilograms (kg)**
1 kilogram = 1000 **grams (g)**

Capacity:
1 **litre (l)** = 1000 **millilitres (ml)**
1 litre = 100 **centilitres (cl)**
1 centilitre = 10 millilitres

Thirdly, you multiply to go from large to small units or you divide to go from small to large units.

Examples
> Change 375 ml into l.
> Changing from 'small' units (ml) to 'large' units (l),
> the link is 1000 ml in 1 l,
> so divide by 1000   375 ÷ 1000 = 0·375 l.
>
> Change 0·09 m into cm.
> Changing from 'large' units (m) to 'small' units (cm),
> the link is 100 cm in 1 m,
> so multiply by 100   0·09 x 100 = 9 cm.

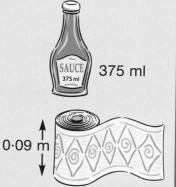

375 ml

0·09 m

UNITS AND THEIR CONVERSIONS

1 Complete the following statements.

(a) There are [ ] grams in 1 kilogram.

(b) There are [ ] centimetres in 1 metre.

(c) 1 centilitre is the same amount as [ ] millilitres.

3 marks

2 Cathy is using a recipe which gives quantities in imperial units. She knows the relationships between the units.

Imperial	Metric
2 pounds	1 kilogram
1 ounce	30 grams

(a) The recipe needs 1 pound of flour. How many kilograms of flour is this?

[kg]   1 mark

(b) The recipe needs 4 ounces of sugar. How many grams of sugar is this?

[g]   1 mark

3 Gary measures the length of his pet hamster. His hamster is 9·6 cm long.

(a) How long is the hamster in mm?

[mm]   1 mark

(b) Gary then weighs his hamster. His hamster is 0·15 kg. How much does his hamster weigh in grams?

[g]   1 mark

4 Whilst driving on holiday in France, Dionne notices this road sign.

Lyon   32 km

(a) Dionne knows that 8 kilometres is about the same distance as 5 miles. How many miles is it to Lyon?

[miles]   1 mark

(b) The campsite Dionne is staying at is 25 miles from the beach. How many kilometres is this?

[km]   1 mark

5 Write 2030 millilitres as an amount in litres.

[litres]   1 mark

TOTAL [ ]

How did you score?

6 or less – try again!
7 or 8 – nearly there!
9 or 10 – well done!

USING UNITS

What you need to know

1 Suggest suitable units to estimate and measure quantities of length, mass or capacity.

2 Suggest suitable measuring equipment for measuring quantities of length, mass or capacity.

3 Read scales on measuring equipment to the nearest division.

ESTIMATING QUANTITIES

- To be able to **estimate** the **length**, **mass** or **capacity** of a quantity, it is useful to have some idea of how amounts in different units look or feel.

  1 mm is about the size of a pin head
  1 cm is about the width of a fingernail
  1 m is about the length of a large stride

  1 g is about the mass of a chocolate bean
  100 g is about the mass of an apple
  1 kg is the mass of a bag of sugar

  1 ml is about the size of a large drop of water
  1 litre is about the size of a bottle of fizzy drink

  By comparing unknown quantities with familiar objects it is possible to make sensible estimates using suitable units.

MEASURING EQUIPMENT

- The equipment you use to **measure** different quantities will first of all depend on whether it is a length, mass or capacity and then on how big or small that quantity is.

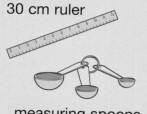

30 cm ruler

measuring spoons

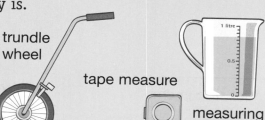

trundle wheel

tape measure

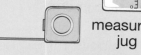

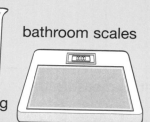

measuring jug

bathroom scales

kitchen scales

READING SCALES

- To read a **scale,** work out how much each **division** (mark) is worth before taking the reading.

Notice that each 100 ml is divided into 5 parts so each part must be 100 divided by 5, that is 20 ml.

1 Join the objects to their correct masses.

| 105 g | 1 kg | 5 g | 30 g |

2 marks

2 360 ml of milk is poured into a measuring jug.

(a) Draw the level of milk in the jug.

1 mark

(b) Some of the milk is poured out of the jug.
How much milk is left in the jug?

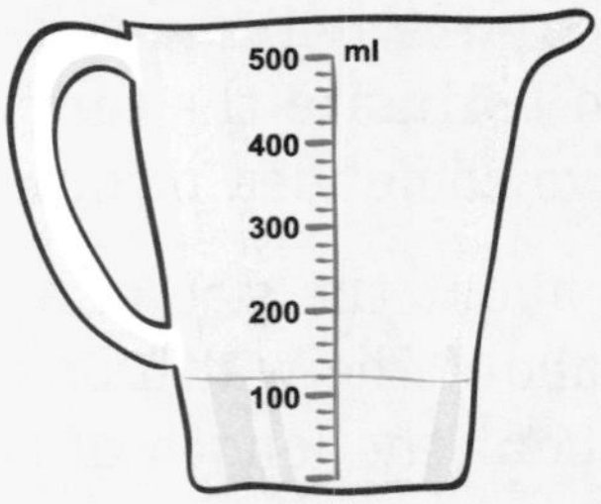

1 mark

3 Shelley has weighed out some flour on a set of kitchen scales. The scales can be used to measure in grams or ounces.

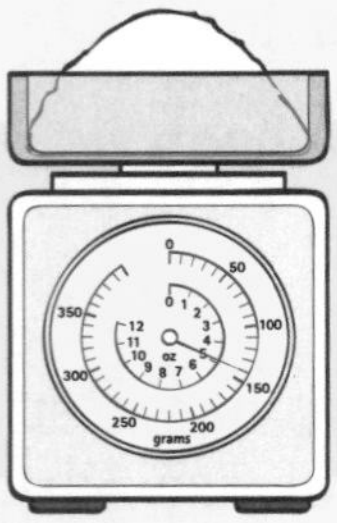

(a) How many grams (g) does the flour weigh?

| g |

(b) How many ounces (oz) does the flour weigh?

| oz |

2 marks

4 Look at this rectangle.

(a) Use a ruler to measure the longer side in cm.

| cm |

1 mark

(b) Use a ruler to measure the shorter side in mm.

| mm |

1 mark

5 Put these lengths in order starting with the smallest.

38 cm   300 mm   0·31 m   30·8 cm

Correct order: [   ] [   ] [   ] [   ]

2 marks

TOTAL [   ]

How did you score?

6 or less – try again!
7 or 8 – nearly there!
9 or 10 – well done!

MEASURES PROBLEMS

What you need to know

1 Choose the correct operation to solve problems involving length, mass and capacity.

2 Record solutions to problems using numbers, units and signs.

3 Explain in words the method used to solve a problem.

WORKING WITH UNITS

- Some problems we meet in everyday life involve working with units. Apply the same rules you use for solving number problems but remember: **always work in the same units**.

Example

Adrian is making bread. He has bought a 2 kg bag of flour. He uses 375 g.
How much flour is left?

First of all, this is a subtraction problem in which the amount of flour used (375 g) is taken away from the amount Adrian started with (2 kg).
But you can't simply do the calculation 2 – 375!
This is because the amount at the start is in kilograms and the amount used is in grams.
Both amounts must be in the same units before the calculation is carried out.

> **Remember**
> - Identify the quantities to be used.
> - Change the units of one or more quantities so that they are all the same.
> - Read the problem carefully and decide whether to use +, –, x or ÷.
> - Give your answer in the correct units.

Either change 2 kg into 2000 g, **both in grams**
then calculate 2000 – 375 = 1625 g.

Or change 375 g into 0·375g, **both in kilograms**
then calculate 2 – 0·375 = 1·625 kg.

Example

Victoria walks 1·3 km, then runs 850 m.
How far has she travelled altogether?

First of all, this is an addition problem in which the two distances are added together. But you can't simply do the calculation 1·3 + 850 because the distance walked is in kilometres and the distance run is in metres. Both amounts must have the same units.

Either change 1·3 km into 1300 m, **both in metres**
then calculate 1300 + 850 = 2150.

Or change 850 m into 0·85 km, **both in kilometres**
then calculate 1·3 + 0·85 = 2·15 km.

MEASURES PROBLEMS

1 Leanne buys a 2-litre bottle of lemonade.
She pours out the lemonade to fill 8 glasses.

(a) How much lemonade does each glass contain?
Give your answer in millilitres.

| ml |

(b) How much lemonade is there in 4 glasses?
Give your answer in litres.

| l |

2 Krispy Pops breakfast cereal is normally sold in packets of 380 g.
As a special offer, packets now contain 50% extra free.

How much cereal is in the special offer packet?

| g |

3 Joshua's father wants to put a decorative paper border
around the living room.
The perimeter of the room is 17 m.
Each roll of paper border is 4·5 m long.

(a) How many rolls does Joshua's father need to buy?

| rolls |

(b) What length of border will be left over?

| m |

4 Kerry is running around the running track.
One lap of the track is 400 metres.
She completes four laps.

(a) How far has she run?

| metres |

(b) Jade is also running around the track. She ran a total
distance of 2·8 km. How many laps did she run?

Show your **working**. You may get a mark.

5 Gary uses an old fashioned tape measure to measure the length of the desk.
The length of the desk is 36 inches.
Gary knows that 1 inch is about 2·5 cm.

What is the length of the desk in cm?

| cm |

TOTAL

How did you score?

6 or less – try again!
7 or 8 – nearly there!
9 or 10 – well done!

EQUIVALENT FRACTIONS

What you need to know

1 Recognize and make equivalent fractions.

2 Compare and order fractions by changing them to have a common denominator (same number on the bottom).

3 Reduce a fraction to an equivalent one by 'cancelling'.

4 Convert between improper fractions and mixed numbers.

EQUIVALENT FRACTIONS

- **Equivalent fractions** are different fractions which represent the same amount.

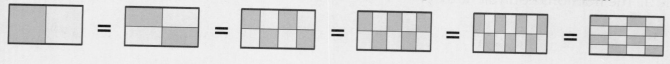

$$\frac{1}{2} \quad = \quad \frac{2}{4} \quad = \quad \frac{4}{8} \quad = \quad \frac{5}{10} \quad = \quad \frac{7}{14} \quad = \quad \frac{8}{16}$$

COMPARING FRACTIONS

- To compare fractions with different denominators, they need to be changed to have the same denominator.

Example   Which is greater, $\frac{3}{4}$ or $\frac{4}{5}$?

change $\frac{3}{4}$ to $\frac{15}{20}$ (multiply both numbers by 5)

change $\frac{4}{5}$ to $\frac{16}{20}$ (multiply both numbers by 4)

$\frac{16}{20} > \frac{15}{20}$ so $\frac{4}{5} > \frac{3}{4}$

> **Fraction facts**
>
> numerator ——— $\frac{7}{9}$
> denominator ———

CANCELLING FRACTIONS

- Some fractions can be '**cancelled**' by dividing the numerator and denominator by the same number. $\frac{15}{35}$ divide both by 5 to give $\frac{3}{7}$

IMPROPER AND MIXED FRACTIONS

- An **improper fraction** has a numerator that is larger than the denominator.
- A **mixed number** is made up of a whole number and a fraction.
- An improper fraction can be changed to a mixed number by taking out as many 'whole numbers' as possible.
- A mixed number can be changed to an improper fraction.

$\frac{11}{2}$ the numerator is greater than the denominator

$\text{whole number} \rightarrow 5\frac{1}{2} \leftarrow \text{fraction}$ this means $5 + \frac{1}{2}$

$\frac{13}{5} = \frac{5}{5} + \frac{5}{5} + \frac{3}{5} = 1 + 1 + \frac{3}{5} = 2\frac{3}{5}$

$3\frac{2}{3} = 1 + 1 + 1 + \frac{2}{3} = \frac{3}{3} + \frac{3}{3} + \frac{3}{3} + \frac{2}{3} = \frac{11}{3}$

EQUIVALENT FRACTIONS

1 Part of the shape below is shaded dark blue.

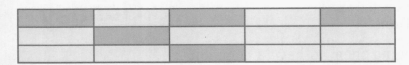

Answer the following, giving your fractions in their simplest form.

(a)   What fraction of the shape is dark blue?

(b)   What fraction of the shape is light blue?

1 mark

2 Circle all the fractions equivalent to $\frac{1}{2}$.

$\frac{4}{6}$ $\frac{5}{10}$ $\frac{18}{36}$ $\frac{9}{16}$ $\frac{7}{12}$

1 mark

3 Complete these equivalent fractions.

$\frac{5}{8} = \frac{\Box}{16}$ $\frac{3}{4} = \frac{6}{\Box}$ $\frac{3}{10} = \frac{\Box}{100}$

3 marks

4 Change these improper fractions into their equivalent mixed numbers.

$\frac{9}{4}$ ☐ $\frac{18}{5}$ ☐

2 marks

5 (a)   Which is smaller, $\frac{2}{3}$ or $\frac{7}{10}$?

(b)   Explain how you know.

_____

_____

1 mark

_____

6 Put these fractions in order from smallest to largest.

$\frac{1}{2}$ $\frac{3}{4}$ $\frac{7}{8}$ $\frac{5}{8}$ $\frac{10}{12}$

☐ ☐ ☐ ☐ ☐   *2 marks*

TOTAL ☐

FRACTIONS OF QUANTITIES

What you need to know

1 Understand that finding fractions of amounts uses division skills.

2 Find a fraction of a number or quantity.

UNIT FRACTIONS - DIVIDE

- **Fractions**, such as $\frac{1}{2}$, $\frac{1}{3}$, $\frac{1}{4}$, $\frac{1}{5}$, i.e. those with a **numerator** of 1, are called **unit fractions**.
- To find a unit fraction of a number or quantity, **divide** by the **denominator**.

Examples   To find $\frac{1}{5}$ of £40,
just calculate £40 ÷ 5 = £8.

To find $\frac{1}{8}$ of 320 kg,
just calculate 320 kg ÷ 8 = 40 kg.

OTHER FRACTIONS - DIVIDE THEN MULTIPLY

- For other fractions, find the unit fraction first,
then **multiply** your answer by the numerator.

Examples   To find $\frac{3}{5}$ of £40:
$\frac{1}{5}$ of £40 is £8 (£40 ÷ 5 = £8),
so $\frac{3}{5}$ must be 3 times this answer, 3 x £8 = £24.

To find $\frac{5}{8}$ of 320 kg:
$\frac{1}{8}$ of 320 kg is 40 kg (320 kg ÷ 8 = 40 kg),
so $\frac{5}{8}$ must be 5 times this answer, 5 x 40 kg = 200 kg.

Quick Tip!

A division of one number by another may also be written as a fraction.

Example 3 bars of chocolate shared amongst 5 friends can be written as 3 ⊃ 5 or $\frac{3}{5}$. That means each friend will get $\frac{3}{5}$ of a bar of chocolate.
9 bars shared amongst 4 friends can be written as 9 ⊃ 4 or $\frac{9}{4}$.
That means each friend will get $\frac{9}{4}$ or $2\frac{1}{4}$ bars.

Remember
To find a fraction of an amount, divide the amount by the denominator and then multiply by the numerator.

Example To find $\frac{3}{4}$ of an amount, divide the amount by 4, then multiply by 3.

FRACTIONS OF QUANTITIES

1 How many halves are there in $3\frac{1}{2}$?

[ ] *1 mark*

2 Kelvin has 45 sweets.
He gives $\frac{1}{5}$ of them to Omar.

How many does he have left?

[ ] *1 mark*

3 (a) What is $\frac{3}{4}$ of £200?

£[ ] *1 mark*

(b) Explain how you worked out your answer.

_____

_____

1 mark

4 How many minutes are there in $3\frac{1}{4}$ hours?

[minutes] *1 mark*

5 What fraction of a metre is 19 cm?

[ ] *1 mark*

6 What fraction of £1 is 60p?

Give your answer as a fraction
in its simplest form.

[ ] *1 mark*

7 In a pencil box, there are 30 pencils.

$\frac{2}{3}$ of them are blue

$\frac{1}{10}$ of them are red

$\frac{1}{15}$ of them are yellow

$\frac{1}{6}$ of them are green

Work out how many pencils there are of each colour.

[ ] blue   [ ] red

[ ] yellow   [ ] green

3 marks

TOTAL [ ]

MODE, MEDIAN AND MEAN

What you need to know

1 Find the mode, median and mean of a set of data.

2 Find the range of a set of data.

3 Collect and interpret data in tally charts and frequency tables.

FINDING THE MODE, MEDIAN, MEAN AND RANGE

- The **mode** of a set of **data** is the **most common** item or number.

Example   A dice is rolled 20 times.

Number on dice	Tally
1	IIII
2	II
3	IIII
4	III
5	II
6	IIII

Tally charts can be used to record results.

The dice landed on the number 3 five times.
This is more than for any other number so the **mode** (or modal number) is 3.

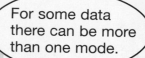

For some data there can be more than one mode.

- The **median** of a set of data, in order of size, is the **middle** value (or halfway between the middle two values).

Example   Find the median age of four children in a family.

7   10   14   15

The **median** age is 12 as it lies halfway between 10 and 14.

- The **mean** is found by adding up all the values and dividing the total by the number of values.

Example   Callum's last five spelling test scores are 4, 7, 10, 8 and 6.
To find his **mean** score, add all the scores together then divide by five (the number of tests he did).
4 + 7 + 10 + 8 + 6 = 35, then 35 ÷ 5 = 7
Callum's mean score is 7.

- The **range** is the difference between the largest and smallest numbers.

Example   Callum's highest score (above) is 10 and his lowest is 4.
To find the **range** of his scores, work out 10 − 4.
The range is 6.

MODE, MEDIAN AND MEAN

1 Louise recorded the shoe sizes of eleven people in her class.

2, 4, 4, 2, 5, 2, 3, 6, 2, 5, 3

(a) Record the data in the tally chart.

Shoe size	Tally	Frequency
2	IIII	4
3	II	2
4	II	2
5	II	2
6	II	2

1 mark

(b) What is the mode of the shoe sizes?   `2`   1 mark

(c) What is the range of shoe sizes?   `4`   1 mark

(d) Write **all** the shoe sizes in order starting with the smallest.

`2,2,2,2,3,3,4,4,5,5,6`   1 mark

(e) What is the median shoe size?   `3`   1 mark

2 Here are the scores in last week's spelling test:

Jane	10	Kevin	6	Billy	10	Rachel	7
Michaela	5	Anne	10	Ben	8		

(a) Work out the mean score.   `8` ✓   1 mark

(b) Here are the scores for the same children for this week's spelling test.

Jane	7	Kevin	5	Billy	7	Rachel	4
Michaela	5	Anne	8	Ben	6		

Work out the mean score.   `5`   1 mark

(c) What do you think the two mean scores tell you about the test?

<u>This week's test was harder, because the results have gone down.</u>   1 mark

3 The mean of three numbers is 8. The mode of the same three numbers is 6.

What are the three numbers?

`8, 8, 10`

2 marks

TOTAL ☐

DIAGRAMS, GRAPHS AND TABLES

What you need to know

1 Record and interpret data in Venn and Carroll diagrams.

2 Display and interpret data in line graphs, tables and databases.

GROUPING AND SORTING NUMBERS

- A **Venn diagram** usually has two or more hoops and is used for grouping things or numbers with the same properties.

This Venn diagram has been used to group the numbers 3, 4, 7 and 9, based on whether they are factors of 12 and/or odd.

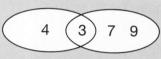

factors of 12 · 4 · 3 · 7 · 9 · odd numbers

- A **Carroll diagram** is a small table which is used to sort out things or numbers with certain properties.

This Carroll diagram has been used to sort the numbers −14, −10, 21 and 50, based on their properties.

	Negative	Positive
multiple of 7	−14	21
not multiple of 7	−10	50

LINE GRAPHS AND TABLES

- A **line graph** is usually used to show how one quantity changes with another. Points are joined by lines.

This line graph shows the temperature between 7 a.m. and 11 a.m. one morning. You can find the temperature at 10.00 a.m. (10°C). You can work out by how much the temperature increased between 7 a.m. and 11 a.m. (11 − 3 = 8°C).

- A **table** is used to store various pieces of data about different people or things.

This table shows some facts about different holidays. If you look along the rows and down the columns you can see that the cheapest holiday is 7 nights in Tenerife (£150).

Resort	Number of nights	Price
Majorca	7	£159
Minorca	14	£265
Ibiza	11	£189
Tenerife	7	£150
Florida	7	£230

51

DIAGRAMS, GRAPHS AND TABLES

1 Sally is sorting whole numbers. She decides to use a Venn diagram.

Write the numbers in the correct sections of the diagram.

12   3   9   18   2   27   4   45

factors of 36   4, 3, 12, 2   18, 9, 18   27, 45   multiples of 9

2 This Carroll diagram shows how some numbers between 15 and 25 have been sorted. Add the numbers 18 and 23 to the diagram.

	odd	not odd
less than 20	19	14, 18
not less than 20	23	22

3 Here is a line graph showing Samir's bicycle ride.

Answer the following questions using the information in the graph.

(a) What time did Samir start his journey?   10:30

(b) How far did Samir travel between 11 a.m. and 11.30 a.m?   1 km

(c) What did Samir do between 12 noon and 12.30 p.m?

Rested or maybe ate lunch.

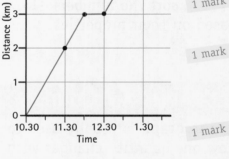

4 The table shows the number of children in Years 3, 4, 5 and 6 in three primary schools in the same town.

	Park Road	St. John's	Westfield
Year 3	23	48	19
Year 4	25	52	18
Year 5	29	56	22
Year 6	28	60	20

(a) How many children are in Year 5 at Westfield School?   22

(b) What is the total number of children in Year 6 at the three schools?   108

(c) How many more children are in Year 3 at St. John's than in Westfield?

31

TOTAL

CHARTS

What you need to know

1 Display and interpret data in bar charts, simple pie charts and pictograms.

USING A BAR CHART

- On this bar chart, the height of each bar shows the number of marks each child gained in a maths test.

  You can see that Karim scored the most and Vincent scored the least because these are the tallest and shortest bars.

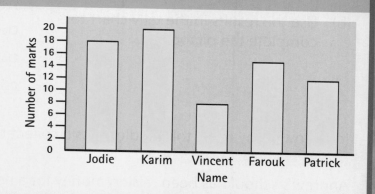

USING A PIE CHART

- This pie chart shows the pets of 20 children. Each slice represents the number of children who have that animal for a pet.

  The slice for Dog is one quarter of the chart. One quarter of 20 is 5 so that means 5 of the children have a pet dog.

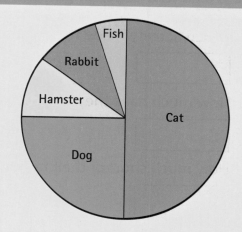

USING A PICTOGRAM

- The **key** shows that 10 packets of sweets sold in the tuckshop are represented by a picture of a sweet.
  Using this symbol we can work out how many packets were sold each day.

  Monday has two sweets so this represents 20 packets of sweets.
  Wednesday has two and a half sweets so this must show 25 packets.

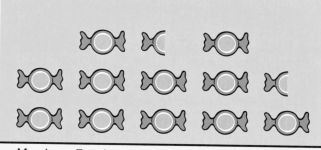

 represents 10 packets of sweets

CHARTS

1 The children in Ian's school are collecting tokens for free books. Ian has collected the data in a tally chart.

Class	Number of tokens	Frequency
3	~~IIII~~ ~~IIII~~ ~~IIII~~ I	16
4	~~IIII~~ ~~IIII~~ IIII	14
5	~~IIII~~ ~~IIII~~ ~~IIII~~ ~~IIII~~	20
6	~~IIII~~ ~~IIII~~ ~~IIII~~ ~~IIII~~ II	22

(a) Complete the frequency values in the tally chart.

1 mark

(b) Use the results in the tally chart to complete the pictogram.

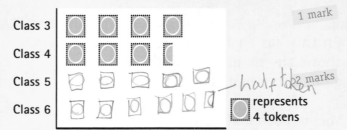

Class 3
Class 4
Class 5
Class 6

– half token 2 marks

represents 4 tokens

(c) How many more tokens did Class 6 collect than Class 3?   6   1 mark

2 Andrew's school has been raising money for a new minibus.
The school needs to raise £10 000.
Here is a bar chart showing the money raised.

(a) Which activity made the most money?

Raffle   1 mark

(b) How much have they raised altogether?

✗ £ 5,000   1 mark

(c) How much short of their target are they?

✗ £ 5,000   1 mark

(d) Which activities raised more than £800?   Car Cleaning and Raffle   1 mark

£2000
£1500
£1000
£500
£0

Car cleaning | Donations | Coffee morning | Carol singing | Raffle

3 This pie chart shows the amount of time spent each week on different subjects at Westcott Primary School.

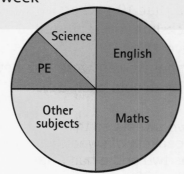

Science
PE
English
Other subjects
Maths

24 hours

Use the chart to work out:
(a) how many hours are spent on English.

6   hours   1 mark

(b) how many hours are spent on Science.

3   hours   1 mark

TOTAL [ ]

PERCENTAGES

What you need to know

1 Understand that a percentage is the number of parts in every 100.

2 Recognize and use the % sign correctly.

3 Find a percentage of a shape.

4 Find the percentage of a quantity with and without using a calculator.

PERCENTAGE OF A SHAPE

- If a shape is divided into 100 equal parts it is easy to work out the percentage shaded. So if 7 of the 100 parts are shaded then 7% is shaded.

- For shapes divided into a different number of parts you need to work out the percentage represented by each part.

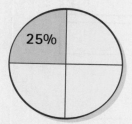

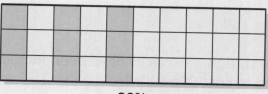

30%

This shape is divided into 4 parts so each part is 25%.
The shaded part is 25% so the unshaded part is 75% (100% - 25%).

In this shape, 30 parts represents 100% so 3 squares represents 10%. That means the shaded part is 30% (3 lots of 3 squares). The unshaded part is then 70%.

PERCENTAGES OF A QUANTITY

- When working out the percentage of a number or quantity, the method you use depends on the numbers in the question.

Examples
To find 30% of 50 m, first find 10% by dividing by 10 to get 5 m, then multiply by 3 to get 15 m.

To find 35% of 6 kg it is probably best to use a calculator.
Enter the percentage as a decimal 0·35, then multiply by 6 which is 2·1 kg.

Quick Tips!

- In percentage problems look out for words such as **sale**, **discount** or **reduced** which usually mean a subtraction will be needed.
- Words such as **profit** or **increase** usually mean an addition will be needed.

Remember
- A **percentage** means the number of parts in every 100.
- A percentage can be worked out of any amount, not just 100.
  - one whole = 100%
  - one half = 50%
  - one quarter = 25%
  - three quarters = 75%
  - one tenth = 10%

PERCENTAGES

1 Part of the shape below is coloured.

(a) What percentage is coloured? [ ] % `1 mark`

(b) What percentage is **not** coloured? [ ] % `1 mark`

(c) Colour another 10% of the diagram. `1 mark`

2 Calculate:

(a) 25% of 160 kg. [ ] kg `1 mark`

(b) 60% of £50. [£] `1 mark`

3 At a petrol station, the prices have been increased by 10%.
Petrol used to cost 80p a litre.

(a) What is the new cost of a litre of petrol? [ ] p `1 mark`

(b) How much will 10 litres cost at the new price? [£] `1 mark`

4 In a box of toy cars 9 are red.
This is 30% of the total number of cars in the box.

(a) How many cars are in the box altogether? [ ] `1 mark`

(b) What percentage of the cars is not red? [ ] % `1 mark`

5 A coat costs £24.
The price of the coat is reduced by 25% in a sale.

What is the sale price of the coat? [£] `1 mark`

TOTAL [ ]

FRACTIONS, DECIMALS AND PERCENTAGES

What you need to know

1 Understand the link between fractions, decimals and percentages.

2 Convert from one to another, with and without a calculator.

3 Recognize and recall equivalent fractions, decimals and percentages.

EQUIVALENT FRACTIONS, DECIMALS AND PERCENTAGES

- **Fractions**, **decimals** and **percentages** are all ways of expressing part of something.

  It is really important that you know all the **equivalent** fractions, decimals and percentages:

$$\frac{1}{2} = 50\% = 0\cdot5 \qquad \frac{1}{4} = 25\% = 0\cdot25 \qquad \frac{3}{4} = 75\% = 0\cdot75$$

$$\frac{1}{10} = 10\% = 0\cdot1 \qquad \frac{1}{100} = 1\% = 0\cdot01 \qquad \frac{1}{5} = 20\% = 0\cdot2.$$

The number facts below can be used to work out the answers to other questions.

If $\frac{1}{10} = 10\%$, then $\frac{7}{10} = 70\%$.

If $20\% = 0\cdot2$, then $40\% = 0\cdot4$.

If $\frac{1}{100} = 0\cdot01$, then $\frac{39}{100} = 0\cdot39$.

Watch out!

$0\cdot4 = 40\%$ not 4%
$\frac{3}{100} = 0\cdot03$ not $0\cdot3$

CONVERTING

- To change a decimal to a percentage, multiply it by 100.

  $0\cdot75 \times 100 = 75\%$

- To change a percentage to a decimal, divide by 100.

  $38\% \div 100 = 0\cdot38$

- To change a fraction to a decimal, divide the **numerator** by the **denominator**.

  To work out $\frac{5}{8}$ on a calculator, press $5 \div 8$ which gives $0\cdot625$.

- To change a percentage to a fraction, write the percentage over 100. $73\% = \frac{73}{100}$

DECIMAL FRACTIONS

- A decimal fraction with one decimal place is written as **tenths**.

  $0\cdot9 = \frac{9}{10}$

- A decimal fraction with two decimal places is written as **hundredths**.

  $0\cdot43 = \frac{43}{100}$

Quick Tip!

Changing fractions to decimals is a very useful way of comparing the size of fractions.

Which is greater, $\frac{5}{8}$ or $\frac{3}{5}$?
Change both to decimals:
$\frac{5}{8} = 0\cdot625$ and $\frac{3}{5} = 0\cdot6$.
Since $0\cdot625 > 0\cdot6$, then $\frac{5}{8} > \frac{3}{5}$
so $\frac{5}{8}$ is greater!

FRACTIONS, DECIMALS AND PERCENTAGES

1 Complete the number sentences.

(a) 25% = 0·25 = [ ]

(b) 30% = [ ] = $\frac{3}{10}$

2 Put a ring around the percentage which is equal to 0·35.

3·5% $3\frac{1}{2}$ %

35% 350%

3 Put a ring around the decimal fraction which is equal to $\frac{7}{100}$.

0·7 0·07

7·0 7·1

4 Change 40% to a decimal and a fraction (in its simplest form).

decimal [ ]

fraction [ ]

5 Use a calculator to change the following fractions to decimal fractions.

$\frac{1}{8}$ [ ]

$\frac{3}{16}$ [ ]

6 Put in the correct signs: <, > or = to complete these number sentences.

0·35 [ ] 35%

$\frac{1}{4}$ [ ] 0·2

TOTAL [ ]

How did you score?

6 or less – try again!
7 or 8 – nearly there!
9 or 10 – well done!

RATIO AND PROPORTION

What you need to know

1 Understand the difference between ratio and proportion.

2 Write the relationship between two quantities as a ratio and as a proportion of a whole.

RATIO AND PROPORTION

- A **ratio** compares one part with another. Ratios can be used in real-life situations, e.g. to increase the amount of ingredients in a recipe.
- A **proportion** compares an amount to the **whole**. Proportions of amounts may be expressed as fractions of the whole.

Look at these tubes of sweets.

The ratio of red to green sweets is 1 red for every 1 green. (This is sometimes written as 1:1.)
The proportion of red sweets is 4 out of 8 are red, or $\frac{4}{8}$ are red or, in its simplest form, $\frac{1}{2}$ are red.

The ratio of red to green sweets is 1 red for every 2 green. (This is sometimes written as 1:2.)
The proportion of red sweets is 3 out of 9 are red, or $\frac{3}{9}$ are red or, in its simplest form, $\frac{1}{3}$ are red.
This also means that $\frac{2}{3}$ are green.

SOLVING PROBLEMS

If it takes 1 tin of green paint to 3 tins of white to make pale green paint, how many tins of white are needed for 4 green?

$4 \times 3 = 12$ tins

If a total of 12 tins of paint are used, how many are green/white?

1 green for 3 white   total of 4 tins
2 green for 6 white   total of 8 tins
3 green for 9 white   total of 12 tins

- Recipes are written to make a certain quantity of food.

Using the recipe opposite, what quantities are needed to make 4 biscuits?
Halve each quantity to give 25 g, 50 g, 75 g.

If 150 g of sugar is used, how much butter and flour are used?
150 g is 3 x 50 g so multiply the other amounts by 3 to give 300 g butter and 450 g flour.

> **Recipe for shortbread**
>
> 50 g   sugar
> 100 g   butter
> 150 g   flour
>
> *Makes 8 biscuits.*

RATIO AND PROPORTION

1 Look at these shapes.
Tick the statements
that are correct.

(a) The ratio of triangles to diamonds is 1 to every 3. ☐

(b) The ratio of diamonds to triangles is 3 to every 2. ☐

(c) The proportion of shapes that are diamonds is $\frac{3}{5}$. ☐

(d) The proportion of shapes that are triangles is $\frac{4}{6}$. ☐

2 marks

2 Rachel has 30 sweets which she decides to share with Philip.
She gives Philip 2 sweets for every 3 she gives herself.

How many sweets will Philip receive? ☐

2 marks

3 Here is a recipe for
a cake that will serve
eight people.

110 g of self-raising flour
110 g of sugar
110 g of margarine
2 eggs

(a) How much sugar will be needed to
make a cake that will serve 12 people? ☐ g

1 mark

(b) How many eggs will be needed to make
a cake that will serve 12 people? ☐

1 mark

4 In a class of children, there are 6 right-handed children
for every 1 left-handed child.
There are 28 children in the class.

How many of them are left-handed? ☐

2 marks

5 Look at this shape.

(a) How many blue squares
to yellow squares are there?

☐

1 mark

(b) What is the proportion of blue
squares in the whole shape?

☐

1 mark

TOTAL ☐

PERIMETER AND AREA

What you need to know

1. Measure the perimeter of shapes to the nearest millimetre.
2. Calculate the perimeters of shapes including compound shapes.
3. Measure the area of shapes by counting squares.
4. Work out and use formulas for the perimeters and areas of shapes.
5. Use the correct units for perimeter and area.

PERIMETER

- The **perimeter** of a shape is the distance around the outside.
- It is **measured** in **millimetres** (mm), **centimetres** (cm) or **metres** (m).

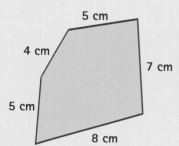

For this shape, the perimeter is found by adding together all of the lengths of the sides. Be sure to include all sides!

4 cm + 5 cm + 7 cm + 8 cm + 5 cm = 29 cm

For more difficult shapes you may need to work out some of the lengths first before you can work out the perimeter.

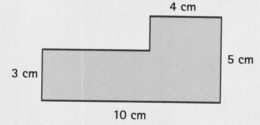

3 cm + 10 cm + 5 cm + 4 cm + 2 cm + 6 cm = 30 cm

Quick Tip!

When you are finding the perimeter of a shape on a 1 cm squared grid, the vertical and horizontal sides of the squares are 1 cm long but the diagonal lines are not.

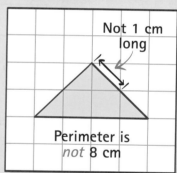

Not 1 cm long

Perimeter is *not* 8 cm

AREA

- The **area** of a shape is the amount of space it covers.
- It is measured in square units: mm^2, cm^2 or m^2.

The area of a rectangle is found by multiplying the **length** and **breadth**:
area of a rectangle = l x b.

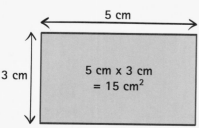

5 cm x 3 cm = 15 cm^2

* Whole squares (2)
* Half squares (4)

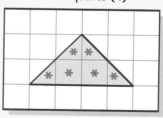

Area is 4 cm^2

For shapes on grids, count the whole squares then make up other whole squares using any parts of squares.

61

PERIMETER AND AREA

1 Put a tick inside the two shapes that have the same perimeter.

10 cm
4 cm

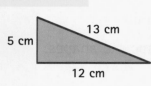
5 cm 13 cm
12 cm

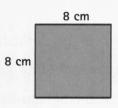
8 cm
8 cm

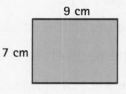
9 cm
7 cm

2 marks

2 On the grid draw two different shapes with an area of 6 cm².

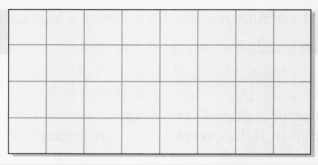

2 marks

3 Calculate both the perimeter and area of the shape.

(a) perimeter =

1 mark

(b) area = [   ] mm²

2 marks

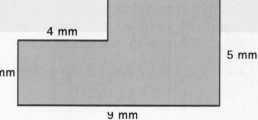
4 mm
3 mm
5 mm
9 mm

4 Jane has made a shape using two tiles.

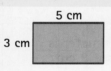
5 cm
3 cm

5 cm 5 cm
3 cm

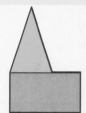

What is the perimeter of the shape? [   ] cm

2 marks

5 What is the area of this shape?

[   ] cm²

1 mark

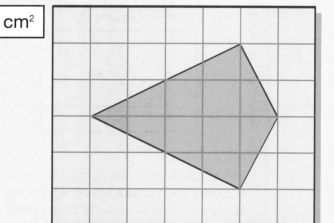

TOTAL [   ]

MONEY PROBLEMS

What you need to know

1 Choose the correct operation to solve problems involving money.

2 Record solutions to problems using numbers, money units and signs.

3 Explain in words the method used to solve a problem.

WORK IN POUNDS OR PENCE

- Some **problems** we meet in everyday life involve working with **money**. You use the same rules as you would when you are solving number problems but you need to be particularly careful and always work in pounds or in pence.

Hayley wants to send her friend a birthday gift.
She buys these items:

The total cost is found by adding all three prices together.

Be careful!

The price of one of the items is given in pence only, another in £ only and the other in £ and pence. You must not do:
28 + 1·32 + 5!
Change the units of one or more quantities so that they are all the same, either all in pounds (£) or all in pence (p).

Either	Write all the amounts in £ and pence, then add them.	Or	Write all the amounts in pence, then add them.
	£0.28		28p
	£1.32		132p
	£5.00 +		500p +
	£6.60		660p now write this as £6.60

If you do this on a calculator you will get 6.6 so remember to read this as £6.60.

DIVIDE, MULTIPLY, ADD OR SUBTRACT?

- As with all problems, **read the words carefully** and work out which calculation(s) you need to do.

Jack is sending out invitations to his party.
He buys a pack of 8 invitation cards for £1.36.
How much does each cost?
Divide: 136p ÷ 8 = 17p
He posts each invitation. Each stamp costs 28p.
How much will it cost to post all the invitations?
Multiply: £0.28 x 8 = £2.24
How much will it cost him altogether?
Add: £1.36 + £2.24 = £3.60
How much change will he get from a £5 note?
Subtract: £5.00 - £3.60 = £1.40

MONEY PROBLEMS

1 Carrie buys some pencils costing 13p each.

How much does it cost for 10 pencils?

[ ] *1 mark*

2 The Post Office sells stamps like those shown below:

| 52p | 37p | 19p | 5p | 2p | 1p |

(a) It costs Bryony 24p to send a letter.
Which two stamps does she buy?

[ ] p [ ] p *1 mark*

(b) It costs Bryony 90p to send a parcel.
Which three stamps does she buy?

[ ] p [ ] p [ ] p *1 mark*

3 For every £5 Jake makes washing cars, his mother gives him an extra £2.
After 6 weeks Jake has made £30 washing cars.

(a) How much money will his mother have to give him?

£ [ ] *1 mark*

(b) How much does he have altogether?

£ [ ] *1 mark*

4 Sam has worked out that $\frac{1}{5}$ of £19.60 is £3.92.

Explain how he can work out $\frac{4}{5}$ of £19.60.
Use a calculator to work out the answer.

_____

_____ *2 marks*

5 A taxi driver charges a fixed amount of 60p for any journey, then 45p for
each mile of the journey.
A group of three friends take a taxi to the station which is 9 miles away.

(a) How much will the taxi fare be?

£ [ ] *2 marks*

(b) The cost of the fare is shared equally
amongst the three friends.
How much will each friend pay?

£ [ ] *1 mark*

TOTAL [ ]

How did you score?

6 or less – try again!
7 or 8 – nearly there!
9 or 10 – well done!

NEGATIVE NUMBERS

What you need to know

1 Recognize, compare and order negative numbers.

2 Read negative numbers on scales including number lines, charts and thermometers.

NUMBER LINES

- On a number line, the further a number is to the left, the **smaller** it is.
- On a number line, the further a number is to the right, the **larger** it is.

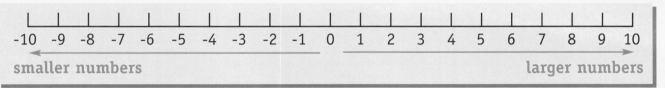

smaller numbers   larger numbers

NEGATIVE NUMBERS

- When counting backwards, after **zero** you can continue into **negative** numbers.
- Some number sequences have negative numbers.

Start at –6 and add on 2.

| –6 | –4 | –2 | 0 | 2 | 4 ... |

Start at 7 and subtract 3.

| 7 | 4 | 1 | –2 | –5 | –8 ... |

THERMOMETER TEMPERATURES

- An everyday example of where you will find negative numbers being used is for recording **temperatures**.

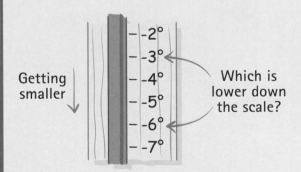

Getting smaller

Which is lower down the scale?

Which is the lower temperature, –3°C or –6°C?

–6°C is lower down the scale so it is the lower temperature.

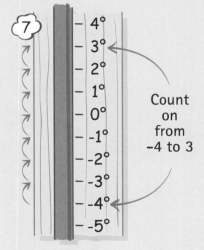

Count on from –4 to 3

The temperature increases from –4°C to 3°C.
By how many degrees has the temperature risen?

Count on from –4°C up to 3°C to give a rise of 7°C.

Grids and graphs
- Another place where negative numbers are used is on grids and graphs.
- Some points can have negative numbers as coordinates. (See page 67)

65

NEGATIVE NUMBERS

1 Put these numbers in order of size.

-10   1   0   -5   -11

☐   ☐   ☐   ☐   ☐   2 marks

2 Put a tick next to the statements which are true.

4 > –5 ☐   –3 < –4 ☐   0·8 < –1 ☐   0 > –0·3 ☐   2 marks

3 What number is the arrow pointing to?

-7   ↓   0   3   ☐   1 mark

4 Write in the missing numbers to continue the sequence.

8   5   2   –1   ☐   ☐   1 mark

5 (a)   What temperature does thermometer **A** show?

☐ °C   1 mark

(b)   The temperature drops by 5°C.
Mark the new temperature on thermometer **B**.

A   B   1 mark

6 This chart shows the temperatures
every hour one morning in December.

(a)   What is the temperature at 6 a.m.?

☐ °C   1 mark

(b)   What is the temperature rise
between 7 a.m. and 10 a.m?

☐ °C   1 mark

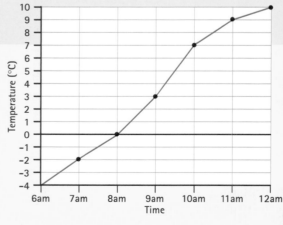

TOTAL ☐

How did
you score?

6 or less – try again!
7 or 8 – nearly there!
9 or 10 – well done!

What you need to know

1 Read and plot points using coordinates in all four quadrants.

2 Know the eight compass directions.

COORDINATES

- **Coordinates** are used to describe a position on a grid. To plot a point from its coordinates, first go across, then up (or down).

On the grid below, the coordinates of A are (1, 7) and those of B are (7, 7).
A and B are joined to form the line AB.

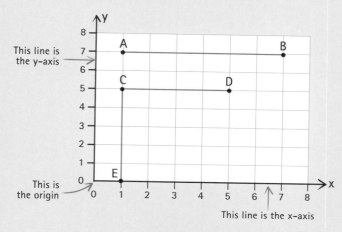

This line is the y-axis

This is the origin

This line is the x–axis

Point C (1, 5) and point D (5, 5) are plotted and joined to form the line CD. The line CD is parallel to the line AB. Another point E with coordinates (1, 0) is added. If a line is drawn to join points C and E it will form a line which is perpendicular to line CD.

- Two lines that cross each other are called **intersecting** lines.
- The **x and y axes** can be extended into negative numbers to produce a grid with four areas or **quadrants**.

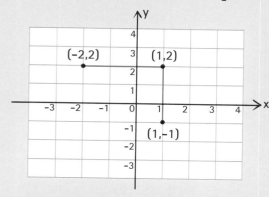

What are the coordinates of the point which must be added to make a square?
The answer is (–2, –1).

POINTS OF THE COMPASS

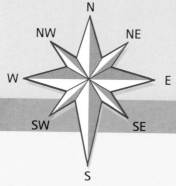

- The eight compass directions are N, NE, E, SE, S, SW, W, NW.
- Compass points can be used to give directions to get from one place to another.

There are 45° between each point.

POSITION AND DIRECTION

1 Look at the map.

(a) Write the coordinates of the Bus Stop.

   1 mark

(b) Which feature has the coordinates (43, 16)?

   1 mark

(c) Which feature is NW of the Post Office?

1 mark

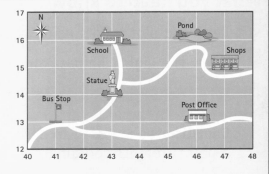

2 (a) Plot the points on the grid using these coordinates.

(3, 5)   (7, 5)   (7, 2)   1 mark

(b) Plot another point so that all four points make a rectangle.
Join the points to make a rectangle.   1 mark

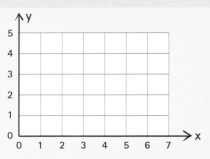

3 Here is a graph. The points A, B and C are equally spaced.

(a) Write the coordinates of the point C.

(,   )   1 mark

(b) Draw a line on the graph that is parallel to the line AC.   1 mark

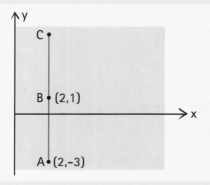

4 Here is a graph. There are two lines on the graph.

(a) Complete the sentence.

Line AB is [   ] to line CD.   1 mark

(b) Write the coordinates of the point where the two lines intersect.

(,   )   1 mark

(c) Join the points A, C, B, D.
What shape is this?

1 mark

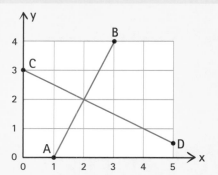

TOTAL [   ]

How did you score?

6 or less – try again!
7 or 8 – nearly there!
9 or 10 – well done!

REFLECTION, ROTATION AND TRANSLATION

What you need to know

1. Reflect a shape in a mirror line.
2. Rotate a shape through a given angle and direction.
3. Translate a shape both vertically and horizontally.
4. Recognize when a shape has been reflected, rotated or translated.

REFLECTION

- **Reflection** flips the shape over.
- A reflection is the same distance as the shape from the **mirror line**.

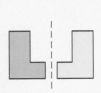  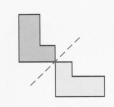

The same shape has been reflected about different mirror lines.

In all three reflections the shape has been flipped over. Notice also that the reflection is the same distance from the mirror line as the original shape.

ROTATION

- A **rotation** turns the shape through an angle.

 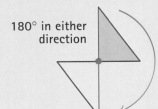

90° anticlockwise

180° in either direction

90° clockwise

The same shape has been rotated through different angles about the same point.

In all three **rotations** the shape has been turned.

TRANSLATION

- **Translation** is a sliding movement: left/right or up/down.

 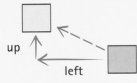

along to the right

down

up

left

The same shape has been translated by different distances and directions.

In all three **translations** the shape looks the same, it has just been moved to a different position.

REFLECTION, ROTATION AND TRANSLATION

1 Reflect this shape in the mirror line.

2 marks

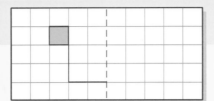

2 Complete the reflection of the shape in the two mirror lines.

2 marks

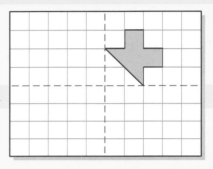

3 Look at the triangles. Complete the sentences.

(a) Triangle B is a [   ] of triangle A.

1 mark

(b) Triangle [ ] is a reflection of triangle A.

1 mark

4 Draw the reflection of the shape in the mirror line.

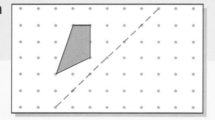

1 mark

5 The shape on the grid is to be translated four squares to the left.

(a) Draw its new position.

1 mark

(b) Write the new coordinates of the point marked P.

New position of P = (,)

1 mark

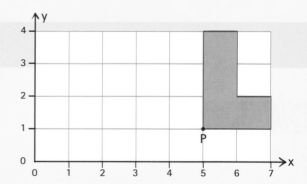

6 Look at the shape on the grid.

The shape is to be rotated through 180° about the point P.
Draw the new position of the shape on the grid.

You **may** use tracing paper to help you.

1 mark

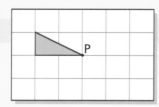

TOTAL [   ]

How did you score?

6 or less – try again!
7 or 8 – nearly there!
9 or 10 – well done!

70

TIME

What you need to know

1 Know and use the different units of time.

2 Read times to the nearest minute on analogue and digital 12- and 24-hour clocks.

3 Use 12-hour and 24-hour clock timetables.

4 Read dates on calendars.

ANALOGUE AND DIGITAL

- This is an **analogue** clock.

  The time it is showing is read as 'twenty to four' or 3:40. If it is morning it would be 3:40 a.m. or if it is afternoon it would be 3:40 p.m.

- **24-hour clock** times are shown on **digital** clocks.

Remember
30 days hath September, April, June and November.
All the rest have 31,
Except in February alone
Which has but 28 days clear and 29 in each leap year.

CHANGING TIMES

- It is important to know how to change a time given in one unit into the same time in a different unit, especially using hours, minutes and seconds.

  A video cassette can record 240 minutes of TV programmes.
  There are 60 minutes in 1 hour,
  so 240 minutes must be 240 ÷ 60 = 4 hours.
  The video cassette can record 4 hours of TV programmes.

  An athlete has run one lap of the track in 90 seconds.
  As there are 60 seconds in 1 minute,
  90 seconds = 60 seconds + 30 seconds
  so 90 seconds = 1 minute and 30 seconds or $2\frac{1}{2}$ minutes.

Units of time
1 **millennium** = 1000 years;
1 **century** = 100 years;
1 **decade** = 10 years;
1 **year** = 12 **months** or 52 weeks or 365 days (366 in a leap year);
1 **week** = 7 days;
1 **day** = 24 hours;
1 **hour** = 60 minutes;
1 **minute** = 60 **seconds**.

HOURS, MINUTES AND SECONDS

- It is useful in everyday life to have some idea of how long things last and which units are the most suitable to use.

  A train journey from one part of the country to another: hours.
  The length of break-time: minutes.
  The time it takes to walk upstairs: seconds.

Quick Tips!

- To change a time from minutes to seconds, or from hours to minutes: multiply by 60.

- To change a time from seconds to minutes, or from minutes to hours: divide by 60.

TIME

1 Draw lines to join clocks showing the same times. One has been done for you.

2 marks

| 11:50 | 7:05 | 10:30 | 3:35 |

2 The time is ten past five.

Show the time 40 minutes later than this time on both clocks.

2 marks

3 Look at the time on the 24-hour clock. Write the same time using the 12-hour clock.

Remember to include whether the time is a.m. or p.m.

14:30

1 mark

4 A video tape plays for 240 minutes. How long is this in hours?

1 mark

5 Two pages of a calendar are shown opposite.

JANUARY

Su	M	Tu	W	Th	F	Sa
1	2	3	4	5	6	7
8	9	10	11	12	13	14
15	16	17	18	19	20	21
22	23	24	25	26	27	28
29	30	31				

(a) On which day of the week does the 14th February fall?

1 mark

(b) Write the date that is three weeks after the 20th January.

1 mark

FEBRUARY

Su	M	Tu	W	Th	F	Sa
			1	2	3	4
5	6	7	8	9	10	11
12	13	14	15	16	17	18
19	20	21	22	23	24	25
26	27	28				

6 Choose the most suitable units for measuring how long it takes to boil a pan of potatoes.

Circle your answer.

    seconds   minutes   hours   days   1 mark

7 How long would you expect it to take a fit person to walk a mile?

Circle your answer.

    3 minutes   15 minutes   40 minutes   1 hour   1 mark

TOTAL

How did you score?

6 or less – try again!
7 or 8 – nearly there!
9 or 10 – well done!

TIME PROBLEMS

What you need to know

1 Choose the correct operation to solve problems of time.

2 Record solutions to problems using numbers, units and signs.

3 Explain in words the method used to solve a problem.

TIMETABLES

* **Timetables** are used in everyday life. Some are simple lists like those found in TV programme listings. Others, like train timetables, are more complicated.

BBC1
6:00 *Breakfast news*
9:15 *Kilroy*
10:15 *City Hospital*
11:00 *Real Rooms*
11:30 *Bargain Hunt*

Newcastle	12:45	13:10	14:00
Durham	13:00		14:15
York	13:50	14:15	15:20
Doncaster	14:10		15:45
London	16:00	16:20	17:15

> **Remember**
> * Identify the quantities to be used.
> * Change the units of one or more quantities so that they are all the same.
> * Read the words carefully and decide whether to use +, −, x or ÷.
> * Give your answer in the correct units.

How long is there between the start of Kilroy and the start of Bargain Hunt?
Kilroy starts at 9:15, count on 45 minutes to 10:00,
count on 1 hour to 11:00.
Bargain Hunt starts at 11:30, count on 30 minutes to 11:30.
The total time is 45 mins + 1 hour + 30 mins
= 1 hour + 75 mins
= 1 hour + 60 mins + 15 mins
= 1 hour + 1 hour + 15 mins
= 2 hours 15 minutes

How long does it take the 13:50 train from York to get to London?
departs York at 13:50   **arrives** London at 16:00
13:50   14:00   16:00

    10 minutes   2 hours

The total time is 2 hours and 10 minutes.

Bob takes a train from Newcastle to York. It takes 1 hour and 45 minutes.
He waits in York for 20 minutes for the train to Liverpool. The train takes
2 hours to get from York to Liverpool. How long is Bob's journey altogether?
Find the total of the three times:
1 hour 45 minutes + 20 minutes + 2 hours.
Add the hours   1 + 2 = 3 hours,
add the minutes   45 + 20 = 65 minutes = 1 hour 5 minutes,
now add again   3 hours + 1 hour 5 minutes = 4 hours 5 minutes.

Always check the units when you are doing calculations with time!

73

TIME PROBLEMS

1 The sign opposite shows the opening times for the local shop.

		Morning	Afternoon
	Monday – Friday	7:00 – 12:00	13:00 – 17:30
	Saturday	7:00 – 12:00	13:30 – 16:30
	Sunday	10:00 – 12:00	closed

(a) How long is the shop open for on a Tuesday afternoon?

hours   *1 mark*

(b) Michael arrives at the shop on Sunday morning at 9:35. How much longer does he have to wait for the shop to open?

minutes   *1 mark*

2 Hassan's watch is showing 3:08 p.m. It is 15 minutes fast.

What time should it show?

p.m.   *1 mark*

3 Zoe wants to tape a film which lasts for 2 hours and 20 minutes and two episodes of her favourite soap. Each episode of the soap lasts for 25 minutes. Her tape can record for 180 minutes.

Will she be able to record everything on this tape?

Circle   **Yes**   or   **No**

Show your calculations to explain your answer.

working

2 marks

4 Here is a train timetable.

Newtown	08:05	08:30	09:09
Banwell	08:11		09:15
Hardwick	08:19		09:23
East Green	08:30	08:51	09:32
Crossley	08:45		09:50
Welling	08:58	09:16	10:05

(a) How long does it take the 08:05 train to get from Newtown to Crossley?

minutes   *1 mark*

(b) How much later does the 09:09 train arrive in Welling after the 08:05 train?

minutes   *1 mark*

(c) How much longer does the 09:09 train take to get to East Green than the 08:30 train?

minutes   *1 mark*

5 This is a rule for working out the time needed to cook a piece of beef:

> Cook for 50 minutes per kg, plus an extra 25 minutes.

How long will it take to cook a $2\frac{1}{2}$ kg piece of beef? Give your answer in minutes.

minutes   *2 marks*

TOTAL

How did you score?

6 or less – try again!
7 or 8 – nearly there!
9 or 10 – well done!

NUMBER AND SHAPE PROBLEMS

What you need to know

1 Choose the correct operations to solve one-step or multi-step real-life problems.

2 Explain methods and reasoning about numbers and shapes.

3 Recognize patterns and relationships between numbers or shapes.

4 Make and investigate a general statement by finding examples that match it.

SOLVING PROBLEMS

- When solving **problems**, read the question carefully and work out the calculations you will need to carry out for each step.

> A farmer has 4 hens. Each hen lays 11 eggs.
> How many boxes of 6 eggs can he fill?
> Step 1 Calculate 4 x 11 to find the total number of eggs:
> 4 x 11 = 44.
> Step 2 Divide by 6 to work out the total number of boxes:
> 44 ÷ 6 = 7 remainder 2.
> The answer to the problem is that 7 boxes can be filled.

> **Remember**
> - Work out how many steps are needed.
> - Identify the numbers to be used.
> - Decide whether to use +, −, x or ÷ for each step.
> - Identify the quantities to be used.
> - Change the units of a quantity if necessary.

RECOGNIZING RELATIONSHIPS

- When working with numbers you begin to realize that there are often **relationships** between numbers which make working with them easier.

> Knowing one fact can lead to others.
> If you know that 24 x 33 = 792, you can also say that 792 ÷ 24 = 33.
> The last digit of an answer gives clues to the numbers used to calculate it.
> When calculating **2**4 x 5**7**, the last digit must be 8 because 4 x 7 = 2**8**.
> The answer is 136**8**.

GENERAL STATEMENTS

- A **general statement** is one which is true for lots of different numbers.
- A general statement, such as 'two odd numbers added together give an even number', can be investigated by finding some numbers that it works for.

> 5 + 3 = 8 ✓   1 + 11 = 12 ✓   17 + 17 = 34 ✓

> **Shape facts**
> When working with shapes you may need to think about all the facts you know about a shape: its properties: number of sides, lines of symmetry, sizes of angles, area, perimeter.

> **Symbols and letters**
> - Symbols can be used to give **rules**, e.g. l x b, 3n, m + n.
> - Symbols and letters are sometimes used to represent rules or missing numbers, e.g, n + 2 means any number add 2 .

75

ONE-STEP PROBLEMS

1 Moin writes down a number.

He multiplies it by 15. His answer is 105.
What number did Moin write down?

1 mark

2 Deena makes bracelets using glass beads.
She uses 20 beads to make one bracelet.
Deena buys 450 beads.

How many bracelets can she make?

1 mark

3 Daniel is collecting stickers.
He needs 96 for the full set.
He already has 58.

How many more does he need to complete the set?

1 mark

4 Ben is thinking of a number.
He doubles it and gets 7·6.

What is his number?

1 mark

5 A group of 108 children
are going on a visit to a farm.
They can travel by coach,
car or mini-bus.

maximum
57 passengers

maximum
20 passengers

maximum
4 passengers

(a) How many coaches would be
needed to take all the children?

1 mark

(b) How many cars would be
needed to take all the children?

1 mark

(c) How many mini-buses would be
needed to take all the children?

1 mark

6 Jenny is setting up the school tuck shop.
She puts out 30 cans of cola, 18 cans of
lemonade and 29 cans of orange.

(a) How many cans does she have on sale altogether?

1 mark

(b) During break she sells a total of 43 cans.
How many cans does she have left?

1 mark

7 The sum of two numbers is 156.
If one of the numbers is 97 what
is the other number?

1 mark

TOTAL

How did
you score?

6 or less – try again!
7 or 8 – nearly there!
9 or 10 – well done!

MULTI-STEP PROBLEMS

For each question show your working out and answer in the box.

1 Erin is doing a sponsored swim.
She needs 60 sponsors to fill her sponsor sheet. Erin already has 38 names on her sheet. 13 friends have also agreed to sponsor her.

How many more sponsors does she need to find?

Answer [   ]

2 marks

2 Thomas wants to send Christmas cards to 50 friends. He buys 2 packs of 12 cards and 3 packs of 8 cards.

Does Thomas have enough cards to send to all his friends?

Answer [   ]

2 marks

3 I think of a number, add 10 and multiply by 5. The answer is 65.

What was my number?

Answer [   ]

2 marks

4 Mr Smith has 12 packs of coloured pencils. Each pack has 8 pencils.
He gives each child in the class 4 pencils. There are none left over.

How many children are in Mr Smith's class?

Answer [   ]

2 marks

5 There are 31 apples in one box and 27 in another. Leonie takes out 13 apples which are rotten. One third of the apples left are red.

How many of the apples are red?

Answer [   ]

2 marks

TOTAL [   ]

77

REASONING ABOUT NUMBERS

1 Write the missing numbers.

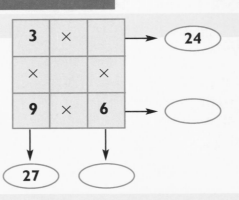

2 marks

2 Write the missing digits.

| | 5 | + | 9 | | = 171

1 mark

3 Here is a multiplication fact: 54 x 79 = 4 266

Explain how you could use this fact to work out the answer to this calculation.
54 x 7·9 =

_____

_____

1 mark

4 Write the same number in each box to make the calculation correct.
You **may** use a calculator.

| | x | | = 256

1 mark

5 In a 'magic square' the totals of the numbers in each row, column or diagonal are the same. The totals are 30 for the square opposite.

Complete the 'magic square'.

16		
6		
8		4

2 marks

6 ,  and are positive integers (whole numbers).

None of them have the value zero. These two statements are true.

 +  = 11   − = 7

Find all the possible numbers that ,  and could be.   3 marks

TOTAL | |

REASONING ABOUT SHAPES

1 (a) What is the name of this shape?

[   ]   *1 mark*

(b) Explain how you know.

_____

1 mark

2 Hannah and Alex have both been asked to draw a shape which has a perimeter of 8 cm and an area of 4 cm². Their shapes are shown on the centimetre-squared grid.

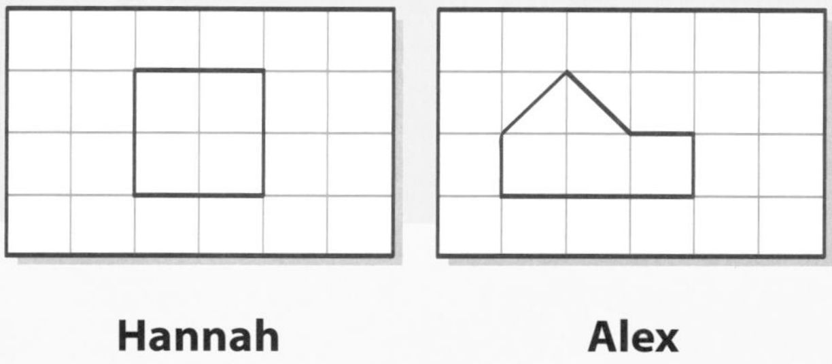

Which shape does not fit the description? Circle either Hannah or Alex. Explain your answer.

Hannah   **Alex**

_____

2 marks

3 Look at this design.

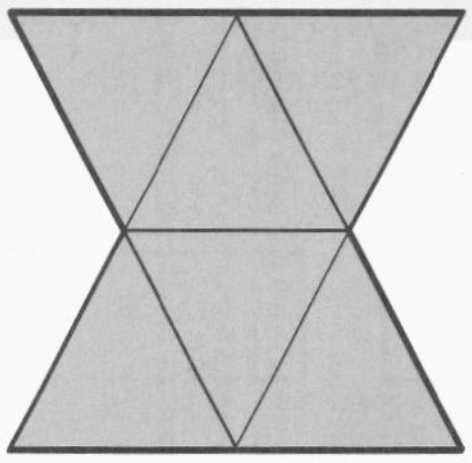

(a) Count all the triangles in the diagram.

There are [   ] triangles.   *1 mark*

(b) Count all the parallelograms in the diagram.

There are [   ] parallelograms.   *1 mark*

4 Draw two straight lines inside the square to divide it into:

(a) 4 squares.

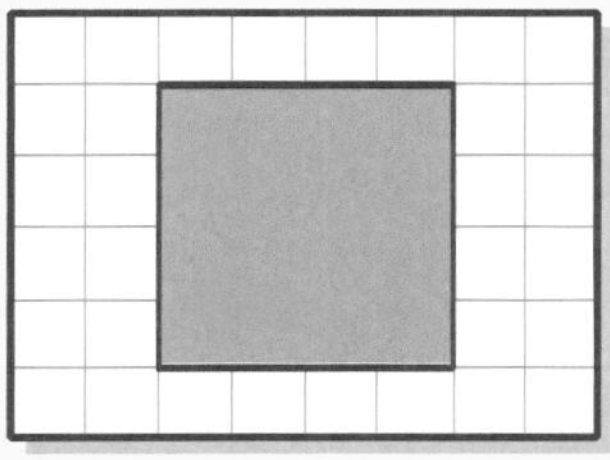

1 mark

(b) 2 congruent triangles and a kite.

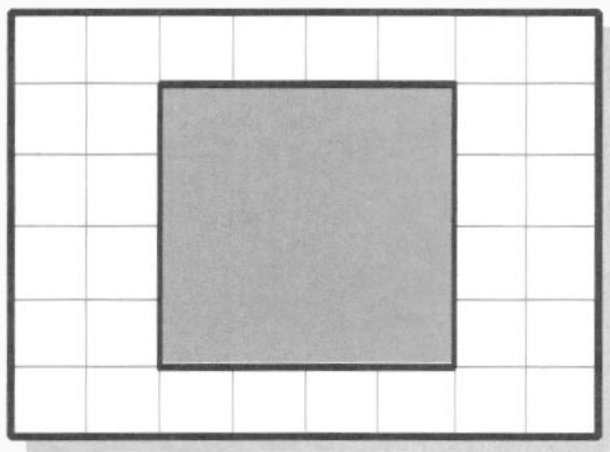

1 mark

5 Look at the triangular prism.

Imagine that you cut the shape in half down the dotted lines. Imagine that you are now looking at the cut face of the shape. Sketch the shape of the cut face below.

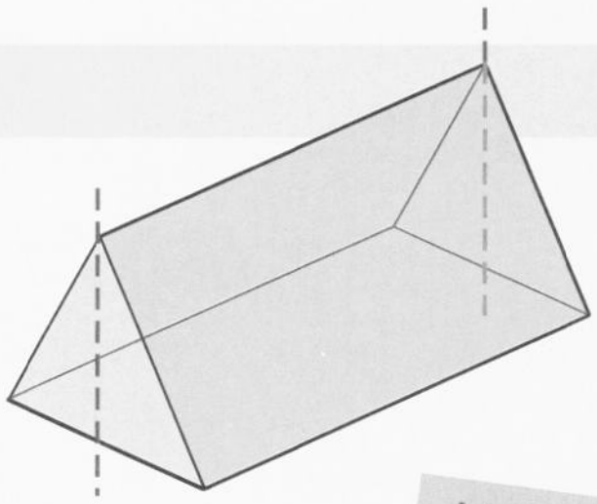

2 marks   TOTAL [   ]

79

INVESTIGATING GENERAL STATEMENTS

1 Oliver says:
'If you multiply a three-digit number by a single-digit number you will never get a five-digit number'.

Use a calculator to investigate whether Oliver is correct.

Circle Yes or No.　　**Yes**　　**No**

Explain your answer.

_____

_____

1 mark

2 Steven says that the sum of three consecutive numbers is always a multiple of three. Find examples to show whether this is true.

2 marks

3 Imran knows that a number is divisible by four if its last two digits are divisible by four. He knows that he can use this rule to work out which years are leap years.

Use this rule to find the dates of four leap years.

2 marks

4 Write the following rules using symbols. Use the letter n to stand for a number. *One has been done for you.*

The difference between a number and 6　　n – 6
(a) 7 multiplied by a number.

(b) Double a number and add 1.

2 marks

5 Complete the table.

m	m + 4
5	9
-2	
	18

2 marks

6 The rule for the sequence 3, 6, 9, 12, ... is 3n.
The rule for the sequence 4, 7, 10, 13, ... is 3n + 1.

What is the rule for the sequence 2, 5, 8, 11, ... ?

1 mark

TOTAL

How did you score?
6 or less – try again!
7 or 8 – nearly there!
9 or 10 – well done!

PRACTICE TEST

You may not use a calculator except for question 14.

Instructions

Work as quickly and as carefully as you can.

You have **45 minutes** for this test.

If you cannot do one of the questions, **go on to the next one**.

You can come back to it later, if you have time.

If you finish before the end, **go back and check your work**.

Follow the instructions for each question carefully.

✎   This shows where you need to put the answer.

If you need to do working out, you can use any space on a page.

Some questions look like this:

Show your **working**. You may get a mark.

For these questions you may get a mark for showing your method.

You may not use a calculator except for question 14.

1 What is the largest whole number you can make using these digits?

0   7   3   7   5

Write your answer in the box.

1 mark

2 Write the missing numbers.

8 x ☐ = 48   ☐ ÷ 100 = 54

2 marks

3 (a) Write the fraction that has been shaded in each shape.

The first shape has been done for you.

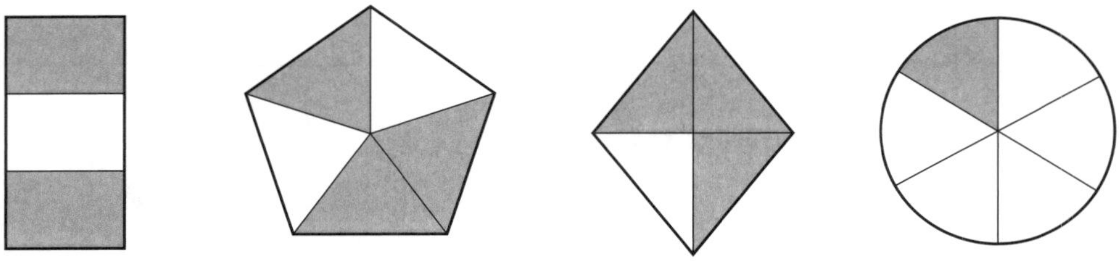

$\frac{2}{3}$ ☐   ☐   ☐

1 mark

(b) Which of the fractions above has the same value as $\frac{6}{8}$?

1 mark

4 Here is part of a number line.

(a) Write the number shown by the arrow.

700   ↓   800

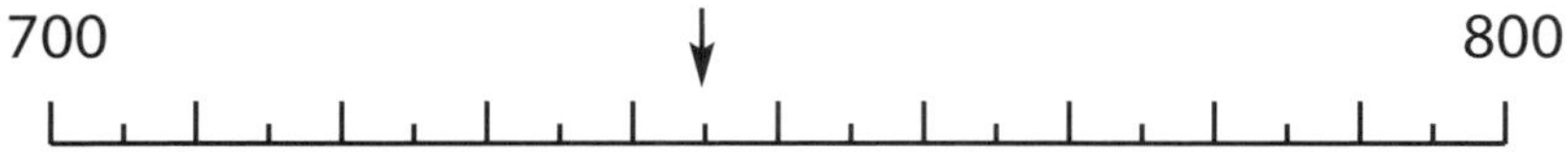

1 mark

(b) Round the number shown by the arrow to the nearest 10.

1 mark

82

5 Look at the shapes.

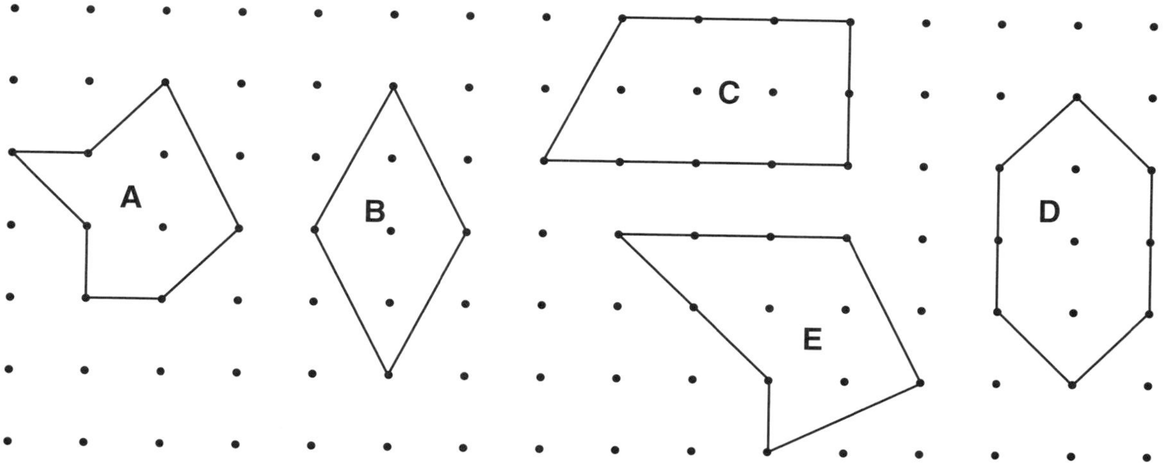

(a) Write a letter to complete the sentence.

Shape ☐ is a trapezium.

1 mark

(b) Draw a parallelogram on the dotted area below.

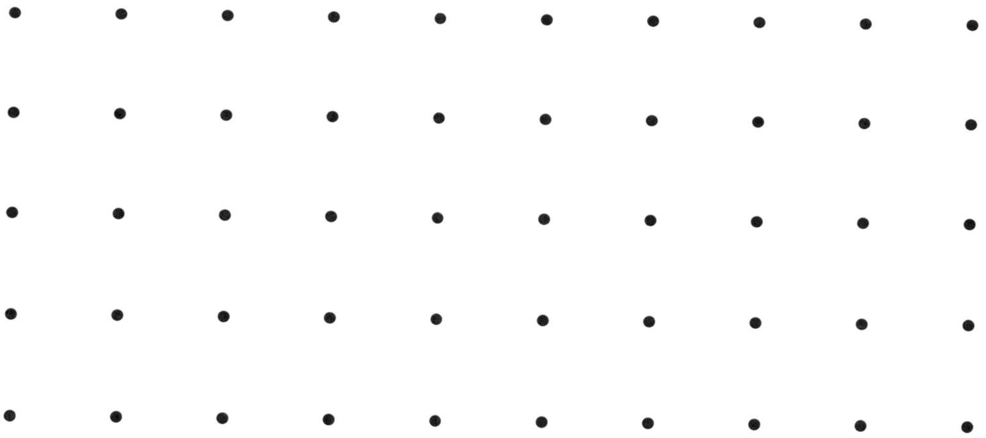

1 mark

6 Put circles around the two numbers which have a total of 70.

50   15   46   10
   24   34   45   26

1 mark

7 Calculate 609 – 345.

1 mark

8 Here is a timetable for the Number 3 and the Number 5 buses.

	Number 3	Number 5
Shopping Centre	8:40	8:47
Mandarin Way	8:50	
Crockett Flats	8:55	8:57
Smith's Wharf	9:07	
Market Square	9:15	9:10

(a) Mark needs to get to Smith's Wharf from Crockett Flats.

Which bus must he catch?

1 mark

(b) How long does it take for the Number 3 bus to travel from the Shopping Centre to Market Square?

minutes

1 mark

9 (a) Nathan runs 12 laps of a track each day.

How many laps would he have run in 5 days?

1 mark

(b) Nathan has done 147 press-ups in one week.
He does the same numbers of press-ups each day.

How many press-ups did he do each day?

1 mark

10 The table below shows the summer and winter temperatures for three cities.

City	Summer temperature	Winter temperature
Newcastle	18°C	−2°C
Oslo	15°C	−6°C
Zurich	19°C	−3°C

(a) Which city has the lowest winter temperature?

1 mark

(b) What is the difference between the summer and winter temperatures in Newcastle?

°C

1 mark

11 Jason has been given £5 to spend on his lunch.
He decides to have fish and chips followed by apple pie.

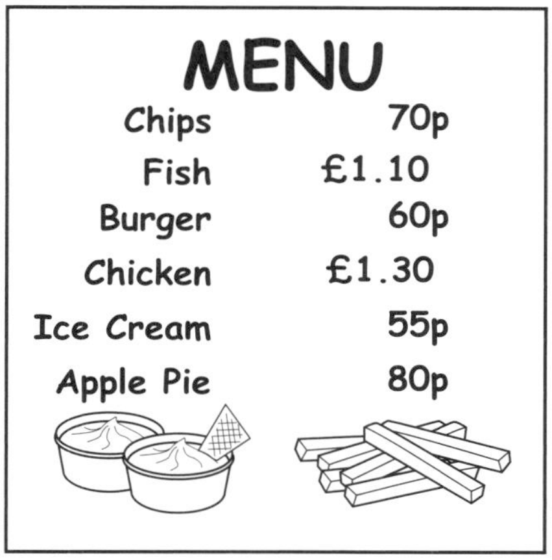

MENU
Chips 70p
Fish £1.10
Burger 60p
Chicken £1.30
Ice Cream 55p
Apple Pie 80p

(a) How much does Jason spend on his lunch?

1 mark

(b) How much change will he receive from £5?

1 mark

12 (a) Lisa is weighing tins of food on a set of kitchen scales.

She weighs a small tin of beans.

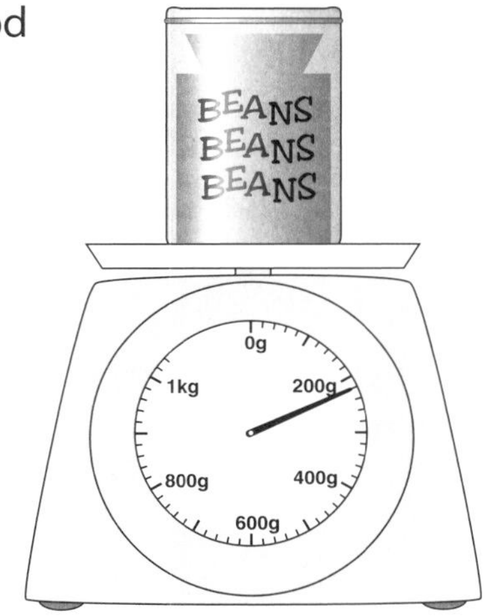

BEANS
BEANS
BEANS
0g
200g
400g
600g
800g
1kg

What is the mass of the tin of beans?

g

1 mark

(b) Patrick has also been weighing tins using a different set of scales.

He weighs a tin of peaches.
The reading on the scales is 0·45 kg.

What is the mass of the tin of peaches in grams?

g

1 mark

13 Draw a line of symmetry on the shape.

You **may** use a mirror or tracing paper.

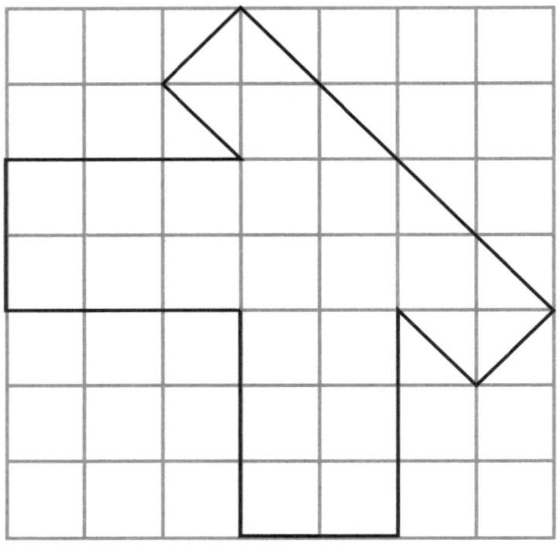

14 The same number is missing from each box.

Write the missing numbers in each box.

You **may** use a calculator for this question.

☐ x ☐ = 324

15 Look at each of the nets.

Put a tick in the box if it is the net of a triangular prism.
Put a cross in the box if it is **not** the net of a triangular prism.

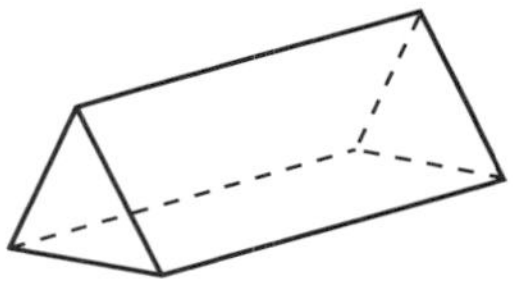

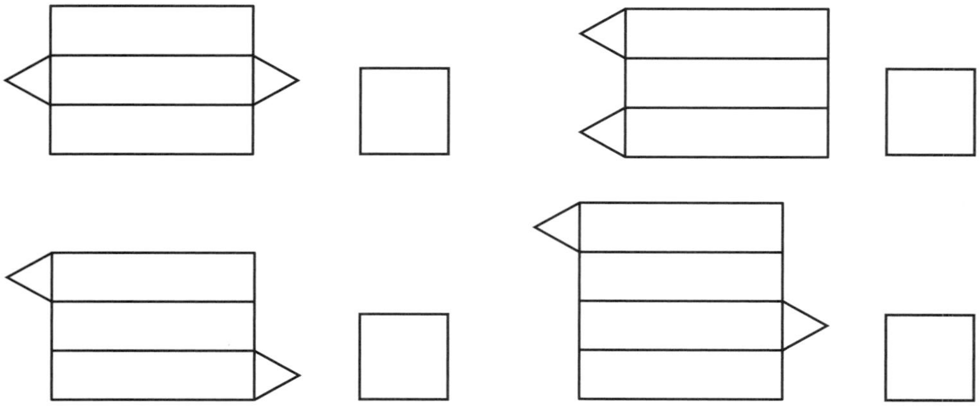

86

16 Here is a kite.
The angles A, B, C and D have been marked on it.

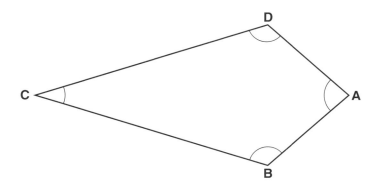

(a) Put a tick in the correct boxes.

Angle C is   acue ☐   obtuse ☐

Angle B is   acute ☐   obtuse ☐

1 mark

(b) Measure angle C.

Give your answer to the nearest degree.   ☐ °

1 mark

17 Here are some triangles.

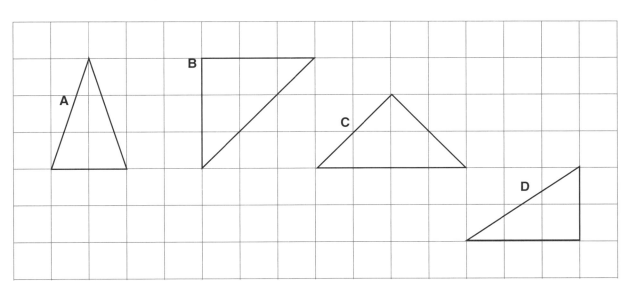

(a) One of the triangles has an area of 4 cm².
Put a tick inside this triangle.

1 mark

(b) Erin says:
'The perimeter of triangle B on page 87 is 9 cm.'

Is she correct?

Circle either **Yes** or **No**

Give a reason for your answer.

_____

_____

1 mark

18 Nasreen has made a sequence of six numbers. Her first number is 27 and her last number is 12.
She has subtracted the same number each time to make the next number in the sequence.

Fill in the missing numbers.

27 [ ] [ ] [ ] [ ] 12

1 mark

19 A coat costs £24.
The price of the coat is reduced by 25% in the sale.
Chelsea's mother buys the coat using her discount card and gets a further 10% off the original price.

How much does Chelsea's mother pay for the coat?

Show your **working**. You may get a mark.

2 marks

20 The pie chart shows how the children in Matthew's class travel to school.

8 children travel by car.

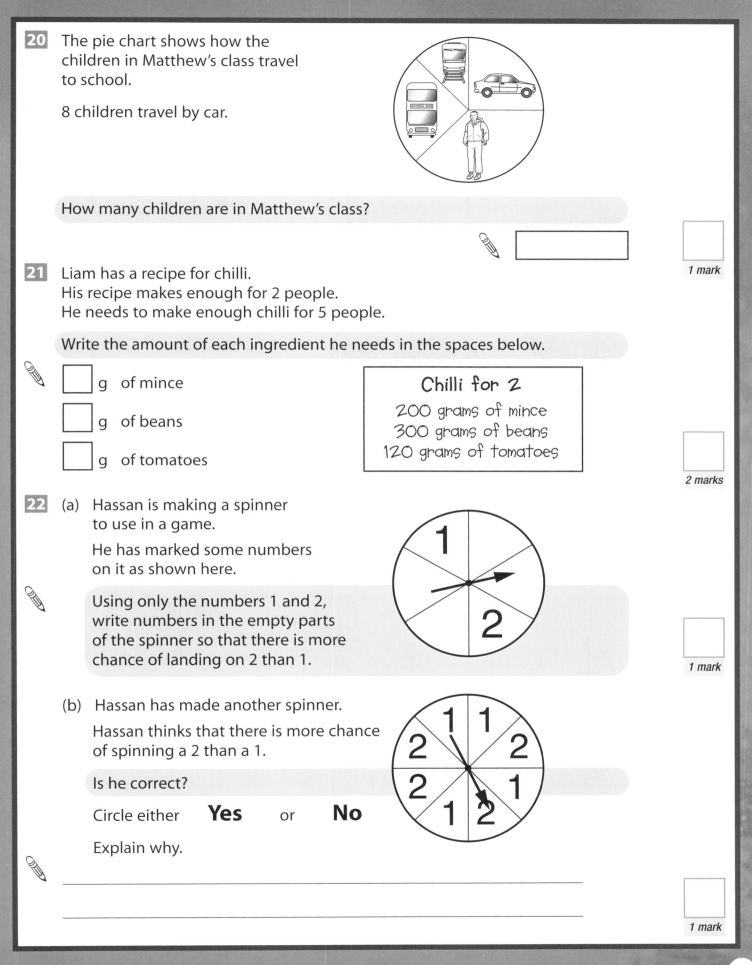

How many children are in Matthew's class?

21 Liam has a recipe for chilli.
His recipe makes enough for 2 people.
He needs to make enough chilli for 5 people.

Write the amount of each ingredient he needs in the spaces below.

[ ] g   of mince

[ ] g   of beans

[ ] g   of tomatoes

Chilli for 2
200 grams of mince
300 grams of beans
120 grams of tomatoes

2 marks

22 (a) Hassan is making a spinner to use in a game.

He has marked some numbers on it as shown here.

Using only the numbers 1 and 2, write numbers in the empty parts of the spinner so that there is more chance of landing on 2 than 1.

1 mark

(b) Hassan has made another spinner.

Hassan thinks that there is more chance of spinning a 2 than a 1.

Is he correct?

Circle either   **Yes**   or   **No**

Explain why.

_____

_____

1 mark

23 The diagram shows a parallelogram.

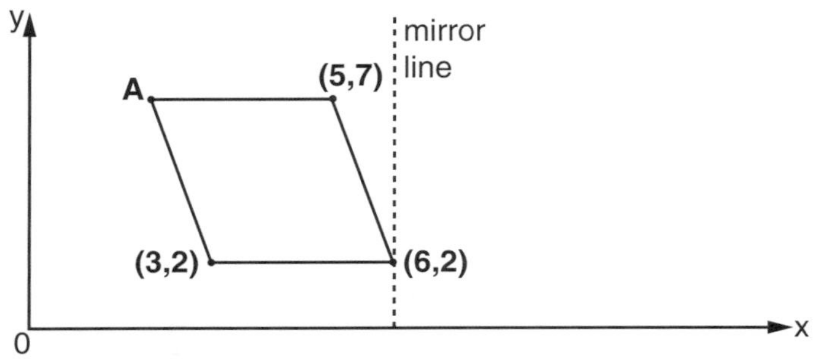

(a) Write the coordinates of point A.

(,   )

1 mark

(b) Sketch the reflection of the parallelogram in the mirror line on the diagram.

1 mark

24 Mia knows that the first four square numbers are 1, 4, 9, 16.
Carly says that all square numbers have an odd number of factors.

Use Mia's numbers to investigate Carly's statement.

2 marks

Total

Possible total of 40 marks

Practice mental maths test

1	What is 19 more than 22?	1	
2	Double 37.	2	
3	The time is twenty to eight in the morning. Write this time as a digital clock would show it.	3	[:]
4	Write in figures two thousand and ninety two.	4	
5	How many millilitres are there in 1 litre?	5	
6	Imagine a square based pyramid. How many triangular faces does it have?	6	
7	What is one quarter of 24?	7	
8	Put a tick inside the shape which is a quadrilateral.	8	
9	Divide 28 by 4, then add 5.	9	
10	Round 1463 to the nearest hundred.	10	1463
11	Which number is the spinner most likely to land on?	11	
12	Write the next number in the sequence.	12	25 21 17 13 ………
13	Multiply 0·05 by 100.	13	
14	Find the total of 1·3, 2·6 and 3·7.	14	1·3 2·6 3·7
15	What is the size of the missing angle in the triangle?	15	°
16	What is the reading on the scale?	16	g
17	A car petrol tank holds 40 litres when half full. How much does it hold when it is three-quarters full?	17	litres
18	Put a circle around the largest number.	18	0·1 0·05 0·3 0·03 0·15
19	Circle the two equivalent fractions.	19	$\frac{2}{3}$ $\frac{6}{12}$ $\frac{4}{10}$ $\frac{8}{12}$ $\frac{3}{5}$
20	In a sale, everything is reduced by 20%. A TV cost £200 before the sale. How much will it cost in the sale?	20	£ £200 20%

ANSWERS TO ACTIVITIES FOR WEEKS 1–8

Week 1 Monday

1(a) 13 157 **(b)** 7·52
2(a) 2·123, 3·123 **(b)** 11·06, 12·95
3(a) 3 units or ones **(b)** 300 **(c)** $\frac{3}{10}$
4(a) 0159 **(b)** 9510
5 Jessica, 8505. *Both answers are required to gain the mark.*

Week 1 Tuesday

1 £11, 346, £13, 146, £13, 416, £14, 316, £31, 614
2 55·0 kg, 5·5 kg, 5·05 kg, 5·0 kg, 0·55 kg
3
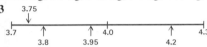

Award 1 mark for any two or three correct and 2 marks if all four are correct.
4(a) < **(b)** > **(c)** <
5 Answers will vary. *Do not award a mark for stating one of the numbers already given in the question.*

Week 1 Wednesday

1 1700, 1680; 800, 830; 1100, 1050
2 656
3(a) 0·5, 0·6, 0·5, 0·9, 0·1 **(b)** 0·89 when rounded to the nearest whole number will be 1
4 136 + 80, 19 x 9
5 Yes; £1.32 is about £1 and £3.55 is about £4 giving a total cost of about £5 for each pupil. There are about 30 pupils. 30 lots of £5 is £150. To gain both marks the answer must be Yes and full working must be shown.
Award 1 mark if the answer is Yes and some working is shown. Do not award any marks if the answer is No. Do not award any marks for exact calculations as this question is testing your child's estimating skills.

Week 1 Thursday

1
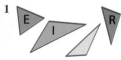

2 ✗ ✓ ✓ ✗
3 A ✓ ✗ ✓ B ✓ ✓ ✗ C ✗ ✗ ✗ D ✗ ✗ ✓ *There are six boxes to be completed. Award 1 mark for any two or three correct, 2 marks for any four or five correct and 3 marks only if all six are correct.*
4
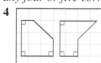

Award 1 mark for drawing a shape with five sides and 1 right angle. Award both marks for a five-sided shape with three right angles.

Week 1 Friday

1

Trapezium   Parallelogram   Kite

2(a) The shape should either be a square or rectangle **(b)** Various shapes are possible. Examples are:
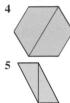

3 C, D, E.
4
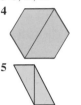

5

Week 2 Monday

1(a) 51 **(b)** 624 **(c)** 16·46
2(a) 21 **(b)** 6, 3 **(c)** 142
3 43, 57 or 39, 61
4 0·3, 0·2, 0·7
5 **4**36 + 4**7**7 = **9**13. *Award 1 mark for getting the number 6 in the correct position and 2 marks only if all four numbers are correct.*

Week 2 Tuesday

1(a) 66 **(b)** 87**1**, **2**54
2 123 – 45
3(a) 362 **(b)** 109
4 1038
5 87
6 19 and 2, 18 and 1. *Award 1 mark for each pair. Allow 17 and 0 to be included in the answer but do not award it a mark.*
7 1·8

Week 2 Wednesday

1

2
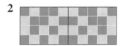

3 B, C. *Award 1 mark for each answer.*
4

5(a) 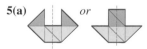 **(b)** **(c)**

Week 2 Thursday

1 cuboid: **6**, 12, **8**; triangular prism: 5, **9**, 6; square-based pyramid: **5**, 8, **5**
2 ✓ A, C
3 D
4 The shape should be a rectangle (accept a square).

Week 2 Friday

1 13·9
2 161·5 cm

3 £179.30

4(a) 0·8 **(b)** 0·6666666 **(c)** 0·625

5 13 m

6 7

7 880

8 13 in each box

Week 3 Monday

1 48, 9

2 5

3 1, 24 or 2, 12 or 3, 8

4 18, 25, 15

5 24

6 364

7 10983. *Award 2 marks for a complete method and correct answer. Award 1 mark for an incorrect answer but with a mostly correct method – allow one error.*

8 18 is half of 36 so halve 648 to get 324.

Week 3 Tuesday

1 301, 308, 315…

2 7, 13

3 16, 36 or 64

4 30, 60 or 90

5(a) The sum of the digits is 18 and 18 is divisible by 3.

(b) The last two digits are 52 which is divisible by 4.

6 2 (on 15 and 30)

7 3, 10, 15. *Award 1 mark for any two factors and 2 marks for all three factors.*

8 21

Week 3 Wednesday

1 21, 5. The rule is subtract 8, or numbers are 8 less each time. *Only award the mark if both are correct.*

2(a) 6 **(b)** 8

3 The second and fourth (i.e. even) numbers end in 0 so the twelfth number will end in 0, not 5.

4 7, 15, 31.

5 19, 25. Add 5 to each top row number, add 5 to each bottom row number, or add on 4, then add on 1. *Both must be correct to gain the mark.*

Week 3 Thursday

1 45º, 135º, 2, 3, 360º. *There are five boxes to be completed. Award 1 mark for any three or four correct and 2 marks if all five are correct.*

2(a) ✗ **(b)** ✓ **(c)** ✗ **(c)** ✓. *Award 1 mark for any three correct and 2 marks for all four correct.*

3(a) 60º **(b)** equilateral

4 The sum of the angles in a triangle is 180º. The third angle is 180º – (90º+52º) = 38º. *Award the mark for an explanation which correctly uses this fact.*

5 70º

Week 3 Friday

1(a) $\frac{1}{6}$ **(b)** 2, because there are more 2s than 1s or 3s on the spinner

2 10

3(a) For 1 mark, fill in 3 or 4 parts with the number 2 and for a second mark fill in the other parts with the number 1. **(b)** No, there is an even chance of spinning 1 or 2.

4(a) Draw the arrow half way along the line to show probability of $\frac{1}{2}$.

(b) 4 black counters (This gives a total of 10 counters, 4 of which are black so the probability is $\frac{4}{10} = \frac{2}{5}$.)

Week 4 Monday

1 24 ÷ 4, 30 ÷ 5

2 4

3 128

4(a) 181 **(b)** 15 remainder 5

5 6

6 14 (2 left over)

7 To divide by 18, first divide by 2 to get 54, then divide 54 by 9 to get 6 because 2 x 9 is 18.

8 7

9 6

Week 4 Tuesday

1 90; 100; 57; 8; 2800

2 3·2

3 100

4 5300

5 15

6 1800

Week 4 Wednesday

1(a) 1000 **(b)** 100 **(c)** 10

2(a) $\frac{1}{2}$ kg **(b)** 120 g

3(a) 96 mm **(b)** 150 g

4(a) 20 miles **(b)** 40 km

5 2·03 litres. Accept the answer if it is given as 2·030 litres.

Week 4 Thursday

1 button 5 g, crisps 30 g, apple 105 g, melon 1 kg. *Award 1 mark for any two correct and 2 marks if all are correct. Deduct 1 mark if more than one object is joined to the same mass.*

2(a)

(b) 120 ml

3(a) 140 g **(b)** 5 oz

4(a) 5·5 cm (allow measurements 5·4 or 5·6 cm) **(b)** 35 mm (allow measurements of 34 or 36 mm)

5 300 mm (30 cm), 30·8 cm, 0·31 m (31 cm), 38 cm. *Award 2 marks if the order is correct starting with the smallest. Deduct 1 mark for each error. Award 1 mark if the order is correct but starts with the largest.*

Week 4 Friday

1(a) 250 ml **(b)** 1L

2 570 g

3(a) 4 rolls **(b)** 1 m

4(a) 1600 metres **(b)** 2·8 km x 1000 = 2800 m then 2800 ÷ 400 which is the same as 28 ÷ 4 = 7. She ran 7 laps. *Award 1 mark for some correct working if the final answer is incorrect.*

5 36 x 2·5 will change inches to cm. One method of calculating this without a calculator is to do 2 x 2·5 = 5 so 4 x 2·5 = 10 then 9 x (4 x 2·5) = 90. The desk is 90 cm long. *Award 1 mark for some correct working if the final answer is incorrect.*

Week 5 Monday

1(a) $\frac{1}{3}$ (unsimplified $\frac{5}{15}$) **(b)** $\frac{2}{3}$ (unsimplified $\frac{10}{15}$). *Both answers must be correct to gain the mark.*

2 $\frac{5}{10}$, $\frac{18}{36}$. *Both must be circled to gain the mark.*

3 $\frac{10}{16}$, $\frac{6}{8}$, $\frac{30}{100}$

4 $2\frac{1}{4}$, $3\frac{3}{5}$

5(a) $\frac{2}{3}$ **(b)** Both fractions can be written as fractions with the same denominator $\frac{2}{3} = \frac{20}{30}$ and $\frac{7}{10} = \frac{21}{30}$ which shows that $\frac{2}{3}$ is smaller, or change them to decimals $\frac{2}{3} = 0.66666666$ and $\frac{7}{10} = 0.7$ which shows that $\frac{2}{3}$ is smaller.

6 $\frac{1}{2}$, $\frac{5}{8}$, $\frac{3}{4}$, $\frac{10}{12}$, $\frac{7}{8}$ (Either convert all to fractions with a denominator of 24, or, convert all to decimals, then compare.) *Award 2 marks if the order is correct starting with the smallest. Deduct a mark for each error. Award 1 mark if the order is correct but starts with the largest.*

Week 5 Tuesday

1 7

2 36 ($\frac{1}{5}$ is 9, so $\frac{4}{5}$ is 4 x 9 = 36)

3(a) £150 **(b)** Divide £200 by 4 to get one quarter which is £50, then multiply by 3 to get three quarters which is £150.

4 195 minutes (3 x 60 + 15 = 195)

5 $\frac{19}{100}$

6 $\frac{3}{5}$ ($\frac{60}{100}$)

7 20 blue ($\frac{1}{3} = 10$ so $\frac{2}{3} = 20$), 3 red (divide 30 by 10 to get $\frac{1}{10}$), 2 yellow (divide 30 by 15 to get $\frac{1}{15}$), 5 green (divide 30 by 6 to get $\frac{1}{6}$). *Award 1 mark for any two correct, 2 marks for any three correct and 3 marks if all four are correct.*

Week 5 Wednesday

1(a) Tally totals are 4, 2, 2, 2, 1. **(b)** The mode is 2. **(c)** The range is (6 − 2 =) 4. **(d)** The order is 2, 2, 2, 2, 3, 3, 4, 4, 5, 5, 6. **(e)** The median (middle number in the list) is 3.

2(a) 8 (find the total 56 and divide by 7). **(b)** 6 (42 divided by 7) **(c)** The first test was easier than the second because it had a higher mean score than the second test.

3 Numbers are 6, 6 and 12. (The total must be 3 x 8 = 24. More than one number must be 6 but all three cannot be 6 because this would not give a total of 24. Two numbers must be 6 giving the third number as 12.)

Award 1 mark for giving two of the numbers as 6 with other number incorrect.

Week 5 Thursday

1

Award 1 mark for five numbers in the correct places and 2 marks for all are correctly placed.

2

3(a) 10:30 **(b)** 1 km **(c)** stopped

4(a) 22 **(b)** 108 **(c)** 29

Week 5 Friday

1(a) **14**, **20**, **22**. *All three must be correct to gain the mark.*

(b)

Award 1 mark if the symbols for two classes are correct and 2 marks if the symbols for all three classes are correct.

(c) 6

2(a) raffle **(b)** £4900 **(c)** £5100 **(d)** car cleaning and raffle

3(a) 6 hours **(b)** 3 hours

Week 6 Monday

1(a) 40 **(b)** 60 **(c)** shade two more parts

2(a) 40 kg **(b)** £30

3(a) 88p **(b)** £8.80

4(a) 30 **(b)** 70%

5 25% of £24 is £6 (one quarter) so the reduced price is £18.

Week 6 Tuesday

1(a) $\frac{25}{100}$ or $\frac{1}{4}$ **(b)** 0·3

2 35%

3 0·07

4 0·4, $\frac{2}{5}$ ($\frac{4}{10}$)

5 0·125, 0·1875

6 = ; >

Week 6 Wednesday

1 (b) and (c) should be ticked. *Award 1 mark each.*

2 12

3(a) 165 g **(b)** 3 eggs

4 4 (Out of every 7 children, one is left handed, so out of 28 (4 x 7) four must be left handed.) *Award 1 mark for recognizing that 28 must be shared by 7 if the final answer is incorrect.*

5(a) 1 blue for every 2 yellow **(b)** $\frac{4}{12}$ or $\frac{1}{3}$

Week 6 Thursday

1 Tick the third and fourth shapes. Both have a perimeter of 32 cm (8 x 4 and 9 x 2 + 7 x 2).

2 Many different shapes are possible. Shapes do not have to use only whole squares provided the total area is exactly six squares.

3(a) 28 mm **(b)** 37 mm² (Divide into two rectangles and work out the area of each.)

4 5 + 5 + 3 + 5 + 3 + (5 - 3) = 23 cm. *Award 1 mark for some correct working.*

5 10 cm²

Week 6 Friday

1 £1.30

2(a) 19p and 5p **(b)** 52p, 37p and 1p

3(a) £12 (30 divided by 5 gives 6 so he will get 6 x £2 from his mother) **(b)** £42

4 Multiply £3.92 by 4 to get £15.68. *Award 1 mark for recognizing that it should be multiplied by 4.*

5(a) £4.65 (60p + 9 x 45p) *Award 1 mark for multiplying by 9 and the second mark for adding on the 60p.* **(b)** £1.55

Week 7 Monday

1 -11, -10, -5, 0, 1. *Award 1 mark if one number is incorrectly ordered and 2 marks if all are in the correct order.*

2 Tick the first and last boxes.

3 -4

4 -4, -7. *Both must be correct to gain the mark.*

5(a) -2°C

(b)

6(a) -4°C **(b)** 9°C

Week 7 Tuesday

1(a) (41, 13) **(b)** school **(c)** school
2(a) Plot the point (3, 2)
(b)

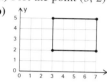

3(a) (2, 5)
(b)

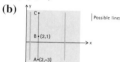

4(a) perpendicular **(b)** (2, 2) **(c)** kite

Week 7 Wednesday

1

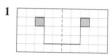

Award 1 mark if the shape drawn is a reflection but is not touching the mirror line.
2

Award 1 mark if the shape has been reflected correctly in one of the two mirror lines.
3(a) Rotation **(b)** E
4

5(a)

(b) (1, 1)
6

Week 7 Thursday

1 Reading along from left 3:35, 11:50, 10:30. *Award 1 mark if only one is incorrect, both marks if all are correct.*
2

3 2:30 p.m.
4 4 hours
5(a) Tuesday **(b)** 10th February
6 minutes
7 15 minutes

Week 7 Friday

1(a) $4\frac{1}{2}$ hours **(b)** 25 minutes
2 2:53 p.m.
3 No; 2 hours and 20 minutes = 2 x 60 + 20 = 140 minutes,
2 x 25 = 50 minutes, 140 + 50 = 190 minutes. The total time of

the programmes is 190 minutes and the tape can only record for 180 minutes. *Award 1 mark for calculations and award a further mark for a suitable explanation.*
4(a) 40 minutes **(b)** 67 minutes **(c)** 2 minutes
5 150 minutes

Week 8 Monday

1 7 (105 ÷ 15)
2 22 (450 ÷ 20 = 22 r 10)
3 38 (96 − 58)
4 3·8 (7·6 ÷ 2)
5(a) 2 **(b)** 27 **(c)** 6 (round up the answer to the next whole number)
6(a) 77 (30 + 18 + 29) **(b)** 34 (77 − 43)
7 59 (156 − 97)

Week 8 Tuesday

For these questions award 1 mark for each main step.
1 9 (First find 60 − 38 = 22, then do 22 − 13 = 9, or, 38 + 13 = 51, then 60 − 51 = 9.)
2 No, he only has 48 cards. (2 x 12 + 3 x 8 = 24 + 24 = 48, 2 short of 50.)
3 3 (First find 65 ÷ 5 = 13, then 13 − 10 = 3.)
4 24 (First find 12 x 8 = 96, then 96 ÷ 4 = 24.)
5 15 (First find 31 + 27 = 58, then 58 − 13 = 45 *award 1 mark for these two steps;* then 45 ÷ 3 = 15 to find one third.)

Week 8 Wednesday

1 3 x 8 = 24, 9 x 6 = 54, 8 x 6 = 48
2 75, 96
3 7·9 is 79 divided by 10 so divide 4266 by 10 to get 426·6.
4 16, 16
5

16	2	12
6	10	14
8	18	4

6 10, 1, 3 *or* 9, 2, 2 *or* 8, 3, 1. Use a method of trial and improvement to find the answer. *Award 1 mark for some correct working.*

Week 8 Thursday

1(a) trapezium **(b)** only one pair of parallel sides
2 Alex. The diagonal of the square is not 1 cm, it is longer, so the perimeter must be longer than 8 cm.
3(a) 8 **(b)** 6
4(a)

(b)

Accept either of the two sets of lines.
5 The cut face is a rectangle. *Award 1 mark for any rectangle and 2 marks for a rectangle with this shape.*

Week 8 Friday

1 Yes, largest 3 digit x largest 1 digit gives 999 x 9 = 8991
2 Examples are 1 + 2 + 3 = 6, 18 + 19 + 20 = 57 (both 6 and 57 are multiples of 3). *One mark for each of two correct examples. Deduct marks for each incorrect example.*
3 Many possible answers. Examples are 1956, 2004. *Award 1 mark for two or three correct years and 2 marks for four correct years.*
4(a) 7n **(b)** 2n + 1
5 2, 14
6 3n – 1

ANSWERS TO PRACTICE TEST

1 77530
2 6; 5400
3(a) $\frac{3}{5}$, $\frac{3}{4}$, $\frac{1}{6}$ **(b)** $\frac{3}{4}$
4(a) 745 9 **(b)** 750
5(a) C
(b) various shapes are possible – accept a rhombus

6 46 and 24
7 264
8(a) Number 3 **(b)** 35 minutes
9(a) 60 **(b)** 21
10(a) Oslo **(b)** 20°C
11(a) £2.60 **(b)** £2.40
12(a) 220 g **(b)** 450 g
13

14 18, 18
15 ✓ ✗ ✓ ✗ *All boxes must be completed correctly for the mark.*
16(a) C acute, B obtuse. *Both must be correct to gain the mark.*
(b) 35°
17(a) Tick triangle C. **(b)** No, the diagonal of a 1 cm square is longer than 1 cm so the diagonal side of the triangle is longer than 3 cm. **The total perimeter is greater than 9 cm.** *The minimum acceptable answer is given in bold.*
18 24, 21, 18, 15. *All must be correct to gain the mark.*
19 £15.60. (25% (one quarter) of £24 is £6, 10% of £24 is £2.40. The sale price is £24 – £6 – £2.40 = £15.60.) *Award 1 mark for a mostly correct method with one error.*
20 32
21 500 g; 750 g; 300 g
22(a) at least three more 2s added. **(b)** No, there is an equal chance of spinning a 2 or 1 because there are the same number of 1s and 2s on the spinner. *Award the mark for an explanation along these lines.*

23(a) (2,7)
(b)

24 1 factor of 1 (1); **3** factors of 4 (1, 2, 4); **3** factors of 9 (1, 3, 9); **5** factors of 16 (1, 2, 4, 8, 16): number of factors are all odd numbers.

ANSWERS TO MENTAL TEST

1 41
2 74
3 7:40 or 07:40
4 2092
5 1000
6 4
7 6
8 top left shape (trapezium)
9 12
10 1500
11 2
12 9
13 5
14 7·6
15 35
16 525
17 60
18 0·3
19 $\frac{2}{3}$ and $\frac{8}{12}$
20 160

Awarding a level for the practice test and mental maths test
There are 40 possible marks on the maths test and 20 on the mental maths test. Double the score from the practice test and add it to the score for the mental test. Compare this final score with the figures in the table below and read off the corresponding level. The marks required for each level are approximately based on those used to determine levels in the KS2 National Tests where most pupils are expected to achieve Level 4.

Level	Score
N	17 or less
2	18–20
3	21–50
4	51–80
5	81–100